Anthony Trollope.   Right Hon. W. E. Forster.
     Abraham Hayward.   Sir George Jessel.

A MEMORABLE WHIST PARTY AT THE ATHENÆUM.

ANTHONY TROLLOPE

A BIBLIOGRAPHY

BY

MARY LESLIE IRWIN

NEW YORK
THE H. W. WILSON COMPANY
LONDON: SIR ISAAC PITMAN & SONS, LTD.
1926

Published September, 1926
Printed in the United States of America

Most noticeable among these personages was a broad-shouldered sturdy man of middle height, with a ruddy countenance, and snow-white tempestuous beard and hair. He wore large gold-rimmed spectacles, but his eyes were black and brilliant, and looked at his interlocutor with a certain genial fury of inspection. . . He spoke volubly and almost boisterously, and his voice was full-toned and powerful, though pleasant to the ear . . . his words bursting forth from beneath his white moustache with such an impetus of hearty breath, that it seemed as if all opposing arguments must be blown quite away. . . He was clad in evening dress, though the rest of the company was for the most part in mufti; and he was an exceedingly fine looking old gentleman.

—*Julian Hawthorne. Confessions and Criticisms. 1887.*

Nothing is more seductive and dangerous than prophecy, but . . . I venture to say that, Dickens and Thackeray aside, Trollope will outlive all the other novelists of his time. . .

And if it be Trollope's fate to outlast all but the greatest of his contemporaries, it will be due to the simplicity and lack of effort with which he tells his tale. There is no straining after effect,—his characters are real live men and women, without a trace of caricature or exaggeration. His humor is delicious and his plots are sufficient, although he has told us that he never takes any care with them.

—*A. Edward Newton. The Amenities of Book-Collecting. 1920.*

PREFACE

Anthony Trollope was born on the 24th of April, 1815, and died on the 6th of December, 1882. His first novel, *The Macdermots,* appeared in 1847. During the period between that time and his death, he produced forty-seven novels, besides several books of biography and travel. He also wrote many short stories, was editor of *St. Paul's Magazine,* and was a frequent contributor to other magazines of his time.

In the following Bibliography, First Editions are noted, with imprint, date and paging, or number of volumes. Those desiring further details concerning the First Editions are referred to Margaret Lavington's Bibliography, in T. H. S. Escott's *Anthony Trollope* (1913), also to Michael Sadleir's *Excursions in Victorian Bibliography* (1922).

Note has also been made of editions which were brought out by other publishers, in the same year as the First Editions, or in a few instances, a year earlier.

Many of Trollope's works appeared first in magazines. Note of such appearance has been made, wherever found.

Also all instances found of translations into foreign languages are recorded.

It may be added that certain of the novels should be read consecutively, as many of the characters reappear in them. The proper order of these is: *The Warden, Barchester Towers, Doctor Thorne, Framley Parsonage, The Small House at Allington, The Last Chronicle of Barset.* These are called the *Barsetshire Novels;* and they are continued by the *Parliamentary Novels,* which are: *Can You Forgive Her? Phineas Finn, The Eustace Diamonds, Phineas Redux, The Prime Minister,* and *The Duke's Children.*

This Bibliography is a revision and extension of a briefer form which was published in four numbers of Mr. F. W. Faxon's Bulletin of Bibliography, running from May 1924 to December 1925. Most of the material has been found in the Library of Columbia University, without which advantage the work could not have been undertaken.

A great deal also has come from the New York Public Library, and the efficient and courteous service rendered there has been invaluable.

Assistance has frequently been given by the Reference Librarians of other New York libraries, of the Brooklyn Public Library, the John Crerar Library in Chicago, and the Library of Congress in Washington.

Several doubtful points have been settled by correspondence with authorities in England and Holland.

All of this aid is most sincerely and gratefully appreciated.

In a work of this kind, filled with detail, indulgence is asked for errors which must have appeared, and any information concerning such errors would be most gratefully received.

Columbia University Library   MARY LESLIE IRWIN.
New York, July, 1926.

CONTENTS

ILLUSTRATIONS

NOTE ON ANTHONY TROLLOPE'S
ATTITUDE TOWARD AMERICANS

Mr. A. Edward Newton has said that it is in this country rather than in England, that Anthony Trollope finds his greatest admirers. If so, it is a well merited return for the fair treatment accorded to Americans in Trollope's writings.

He had always felt that his mother's book, *Domestic Manners of the Americans,* did great injustice to that people, and although, when he himself saw reason for criticism, he, as well as his mother, expressed such sentiments without hesitation and with characteristic vigor, he was now determined to do what he could toward giving out, under the name of Trollope, a fairer delineation of American traits than he considered Frances Trollope's book to be.

My mother had written a very popular, but, as I had thought a somewhat unjust, book about our cousins over the water. She had seen what was distasteful in the manners of a young people, but had hardly recognized their energy. I had entertained for many years an ambition to follow her footsteps there, and to write another book. . . I worked very hard at the task I had assigned to myself, and did, I think, see much of the manners and institutions of the people. . .   —*Autobiography.* 1883.

His book, *North America,* therefore, is the result of a desire to write about a people whom he had tried to know and understand, and it shows a distinctly friendly attitude toward America and the Americans.

Another pleasant evidence of this feeling is found in his novels, where he frequently gives Americans place among his prominent personages.

Plantagenet Palliser, later the Duke of Omnium, is one of the best-known of all Trollope's characters, and his name heads the list of the author's own favorites. This Duke of Omnium represents England's highest nobility, and yet Trollope, in *The Duke's Children,* chooses an American girl, Isabel Boncassen, for the wife of the Duke's son and heir, young Lord Silverbridge, and most suitably and charmingly

9

does she fill that exalted position, as Trollope depicts the situation. Moreover, it was a true love match.

This again occurs in *He Knew He Was Right*, in which a high-born Englishman, the Honourable Charles Glascock, heir to a peer, falls in love with and marries Caroline Spalding, niece of the American Minister to Italy. She also is shown to be admirably qualified to fill the position in which the author places her.

Perhaps the most significant instance of any is found in *The American Senator*. Here the chief character is an American of high political position, and of great intelligence, who is in England with the avowed purpose of studying her institutions. He never hesitates to say what he thinks, generally to the utter routing of his English companions. Trollope invariably depicts the Senator as the easy victor in these discussions, his listeners sitting speechless and glaring at his audacity, while he is opening his mind on the subject of some of their most cherished traditions.

But at the end of the story, we are told, with that quick right-about-face which is one of the great charms of Trollope's style, that:—

A few weeks afterwards, the Senator took his departure for home, and when we last heard of him, was thundering in the Senate against certain practices on the part of his own country which he thought unjust to other nations.

ANTHONY TROLLOPE

I. SINGLE WORKS

The American senator. In 3 vols. London, Chapman and Hall, 1877.

Appeared in Temple bar, May, 1876-July, 1877, vol. 47-50.

Pub. also in Harper's Library of select novels, N.Y., 1877, 190 p.

Pub. also in Tauchnitz Collection of British authors, 1877, 3 vols.

Tr. into Dutch: En vinter i Dillsborough, 1877, 2 vols.

Several of the characters appear also in *Ayala's angel* and in the *Barchester* and *Parliamentary Novels*.

Reviews

Crawley, T. W., in Academy, Nov. 1877, vol. 12, p. 487-488.

Athenæum, June 1877, vol. 51, no. 2590, p. 765-767.

Canadian monthly, Sept. 1877, vol. 12, p. 319-320.

Harper's magazine, Oct. 1877, vol. 55, p. 790.

Nation (N.Y.), Aug. 1877, vol. 25, p. 122-123.

Spectator, Aug. 31, 1878, vol. 51, p. 1101-1102.

Times (Lond.) Aug. 10, 1877, p. 3, col. 2.

Australia and New Zealand. In 2 vols. London, Chapman and Hall, 1873. maps.

Pub. also in Melbourne, Australia in 1 vol. 1873.

Pub. also in Tauchnitz Collection of British authors, 1873, 3 vols.

In 1874 Chapman and Hall brought out this work in four separate parts, with titles:

New South Wales and Queenland, 209 p.

South Australia and Western Australia, 146 p.

New Zealand, 166 p.

Victoria and Tasmania, 195 p.

Tr. into Dutch: Reis door Australie en Nieuw-Zeeland, 1875, 2 vols. 2 illus.

Reviews

Chuck, Thomas. "One story is good until another is told;" or, A reply to Mr. Anthony Trollope on that part of his work entitled *Australia and New Zealand*, relating to the Colony of Victoria, 1877.

Horne, R. H., in Contemporary review, 1873, vol. 22,
p. 699-730.
Simcox, Edith, in Fortnightly review, May 1873, vol. 19,
p. 662-663.
Athenæum, March 1873, no. 2366, p. 276.
Saturday review, April 1873, vol. 35, p. 554-555.
Spectator, 1873, vol. 46, May 10, p. 607-608; May 17,
p. 640-641.
Times (London), April 12, 1873, p. 7, col. 2.

An Autobiography. In 2 vols. Edinburgh and London, Wm.
Blackwood and sons, 1883, port. frontispiece.
The Autobiography was written during 1875 and 1876,
and left in the hands of Anthony Trollope's son, Henry
Merivale Trollope, who published it after his father's
death, which occurred Dec. 6, 1882.
Pub. also by Harper, N.Y., 1883, xii, 329 p., port.
Pub. also in Tauchnitz Collection of British authors,
1883, 334 p.
A 2d edition pub. in London in 1883.

Reviews

Dronsart, Marie, Une Autobiographie du romancier An-
thony Trollope, 24 p., in Correspondant, Dec. 1884, new
ser. vol. 101, p. 1111-1134.
Graham, Bessie, in The bookman's manual. 2d ed. 1924,
p. 213.
Hawthorne, Julian. The maker of many books, in his
Confessions and criticisms, 1887, p. 140-162.
     Same article in Manhattan, Dec. 1883, vol. 2, p. 573-578.
Littledale, R. F., in Academy, Oct. 1883, vol. 24, p. 273-
274.
Mesick, Jane, The English traveller in America, 1922,
p. 13 and 293.
Morley, Henry, Of English literature in the reign of
Victoria, 1882 (written in 1874), p. xxxiv.
Murry, J. M., Trollope in autobiography, a review of
"An autobiography by Anthony Trollope, introduction by
Michael Sadleir, World's classics edition," in Nation &
Athenæum (Lond.), April 28, 1923, vol. 33, p. 120-121.
Rhodes, James F., History of the United States. 1919.
vol. 8, p. 92.
Swinburne, Algernon Charles. Studies in prose and
poetry. 1894. p. 94.
Tanzer, A., in Nation (N.Y.), Nov. 1883, vol. 37, p. 396-
397.
Trollope, T. A. What I remember. 2d ed. 1887, vol. 1,
p. 288; vol. 2, p. 331-337.
Whibley, Charles, in English review, July 1923, p. 33-38.
     Same article in Littell's, Aug. 25, 1923, p. 369-372.

Athenæum, Oct. 13, 1883, II, no. 2920, p. 457-459.
Atlantic monthly, Feb. 1884, vol. 53, p. 267-271: Mr.
Trollope's latest character.
Blackwood's magazine, Nov. 1883, vol. 134, p. 577-593.
  Same article in Littell's, Dec. 8, 1883, vol. 159, p. 579-
  593.
Contemporary review, Nov. 1883, vol. 44, p. 787.
Continent, Dec. 1883, vol. 4, p. 736, 768.
Edinburgh review, Jan. 1884, vol. 159, p. 186-212: Literary
life of Trollope.
  Same article in Littell's, Feb. 1884, vol. 160, p. 451-
  465.
Evening post (N.Y.), Aug. 6, 1923, p. 6, col. 5-6, Review
of *An Autobiography*, by Anthony Trollope, World's clas-
sics edition, London, 1923.
Graphic, Oct. 20, 1883, vol. 28, p. 391.
Harper's magazine (editorial), Jan. 1884, vol. 68, p. 317.
Literary world, Dec. 1883, vol. 14, p. 442-443.
Macmillan's magazine, Nov. 1884, vol. 49, p. 47-56.
Month, 1883, vol. 30, p. 484-493.
Publishers' circular (Lond.), 1923, vol. 118, April 21,
p. 419; April 28, p. 454.
Saturday Review, Oct. 20, 1883, vol. 56, p. 505-506.
Spectator, 1883, vol. 56, Oct. 20, p. 1343-1344; Oct. 27,
p. 1373-1374, 1376-1377, 1377-1379.
Times (Lond.) Sept. 28, 1883, p. 3, col. 5.
——— ——— Oct. 12, 1883, p. 10, col. 1.
——— ——— Oct. 13, 1883, p. 8, col. 1.
Tribune (N.Y.) (editorial), Oct. 20, 1883. p. 4, col. 3.
——— ——— (editorial), Oct. 23, 1883, p. 4, col. 4.
——— ——— (editorial, Cobbler's wax, Sunday, Sept. 2,
1923, p. 4.
Westminster review. Jan. 1884, vol. 121, p. 83-115.
  Same article in Littell's, April 1884, vol. 161, p. 95-212.

Ayala's angel. In 3 vols. London, Chapman and Hall, 1881.
  Pub. also by Harper, N.Y., 1881.
  Pub. also in Tauchnitz Collection of British authors,
1881, 3 vols.
  Several of the characters appear also in *The American
senator*.

Reviews

Athenæum, May, 1881, no. 2795, p. 686.
Critic (N.Y.), July 16, 1881, vol. 1, p. 194.
——— ——— Aug. 13, 1881, vol. 1, p. 218-219.
Harper's magazine, Oct. 1881, vol. 63, p. 794-795.
Nation (N.Y.), Sept. 29, 1881, vol. 33, p. 257.
Saturday review, June 1881, vol. 51, p. 756-757.
Spectator, June, 1881, vol. 54, p. 804-805.
Times (Lond.), July 16, 1881, p. 5, col. 5.

Westminster review, Oct. 1881, new ser., vol. 60, p. 566-567.

Barchester Towers. In 3 vols. London, Longman, Brown, Green, Longmans & Robert, 1857.
This is the second in the series *Barsetshire Novels.*
Pub. also in Tauchnitz Collection of British authors, 1857, 2 vols., xii, 680 p.
Pub. also (with *The Warden*), by Harper, N. Y., 1870, 240 p.
Tr. into French: Les Tours de Barchester, tr. de l'anglais par L. Martel, 1886, 2 vols.
An extract entitled: "Who shall be cock of the walk?" in Newbolt, Sir Henry. An English anthology of prose and poetry. 1921, vol. 1, p. 856-860.

Reviews

Montégut, Émile, Le roman des mœurs en Angleterre, 33 p., in Revue des deux mondes, Oct. 1858, 2ᵉ pér., vol. 17, p. 756-788.
Montégut, Émile. Écrivains modernes de l'Angleterre, 1892, vol. 2, p. 121-138. Le roman de mœurs religieuses et aristocratiques, *Barchester Towers.*
Athenæum, May 1857, no. 1544, p. 689-690.
Herald (N. Y.), Aug. 8, 1914, p. 8, col. 4-6. 1 illus. "Lest we forget." Intimate studies of the great novels of the good old times. Anthony Trollope and *Barchester Towers.*
National review, Oct. 1858, vol. 7, p. 416-435.
North British review, June 1864, vol. 40, p. 369-401.
Public opinion (Lond.), Feb. 26, 1870, vol. 17, p. 265.
Times (Lond.), Aug. 13, 1857, p. 5, col. 5.
———— ———— Literary suppl. March 20, 1919, p. 153, col. 2, Ullathorne Court.
Westminster review, Oct. 1857, vol. 68, p. 594-596.

The Belton Estate. In 3 vols. London, Chapman and Hall, 1866.
Appeared in Fortnightly review, May, 1865-Feb. 1866, vols. 1-3.
Appeared also in Littell's, July 1865-Jan. 1866, vol. 88.
Pub. also by Harper, N. Y., 1866, 140 p.
Pub. also in Tauchnitz Collection of British authors, 1866, 2 vols., vi, 598 p.
Tr. into Dutch: Het huis Belton, naar het Engl. door M. P. Lindo, 1867, 2 vols., plate.
Tr. into French: Le domaine de Belton; roman, tr. par E. Daillac, Paris, 1875.

Reviews

Forgues, E. D. Le roman anglais contemporain: *Belton Estate,* in Revue des deux mondes, 1867, 2ᵉ pér., vol. 69, p. 1017-1018.

Nevins, Allan, Trollope's novels in New York evening sun, The book column, June 30, 1924.

Athenæum, Feb. 1866, no. 1997, p. 166.
Contemporary review, 1866, vol. 3, p. 300-302.
Harper's magazine, March, 1866, vol. 32, p. 527.
Nation (N. Y.), Jan. 4, 1866, vol. 2, p. 21-22.
Saturday review, Feb. 1866, vol. 21, p. 140-142.
Spectator, Jan. 27, 1866, vol. 39, p. 103-104.

The Bertrams. In 3 vols. London, Chapman & Hall, 1859.
Pub. also by Harper (N. Y.), in 1859, 528 p., and in 1866, 140 p.
Pub. also in Tauchnitz collection of British authors, 1859, 2 vols., xii, 756 p.
Tr. into Danish: Familien Bertram, overs. fra engelsk, 1863, 3 vols.
Tr. into Dutch: De Bertrams, 1860, 2 vols.
Tr. into French: Les Bertram, tr. de l'anglais par l'un des rédacteurs de la "Revue nationale," 1865, 2 vols.
Tr. into German: Die Bertrams, deutsch von A. Kretzschmar. 186-? 1151 p. (in Bibliothek europäische).
Several of the characters appear also in *Miss Mackenzie*.

Reviews

Forgues, E. D. Romans de la vie anglaise: *The Bertrams* and *Castle Richmond,* in Revue des deux mondes, 1860, 2ᵉ pér., vol. 29, p. 369-398.
Thorold, Algar, Introduction, John Lane New Pocket edition of *The Bertrams,* 1905.

Athenæum, March 1859, no. 1639, p. 420.
Bentley's Quarterly review, July 1859, vol. 1, p. 456-462.
Harper's magazine, Jan. 1880, vol. 60, p. 314.
National review, July 1859, vol. 9, p. 187-199.
New monthly magazine, April 1859, vol. 115, p. 500.
North British review, June 1864, vol. 40, p. 369-401.
Saturday review, March 1859, vol. 7, p. 368-369.

British sports and pastimes, edited by Anthony Trollope. In 1 vol., 322 p. London, Virtue & Co., 1868.
Eight papers, reprinted from St. Paul's magazine. Only the preface (p. 1-7) and the second paper, "On hunting," (p. 70-129), were written by Trollope.

Reviews

Public opinion (Lond.), Jan. 2, 1869, vol. 15, p. 12.
Saturday review, Nov. 13, 1869, vol. 28, p. 652-654.
Spectator, Jan. 1869, vol. 42, p. 16-17.

Can you forgive her? In 2 vols. London, Chapman and Hall, 1864. 40 illustrations.

"Each volume contains 20 illus., those in vol. 1 done by "Phiz" (Hablot K. Browne), but Frederick Chapman, the publisher, considered them so bad and incongruous, that the remainder were made by a Miss Taylor."—From Escott, T.H.S, Anthony Trollope, 1913.

This is the first in the series *Parliamentary Novels.*

Pub. also by Harper, N. Y., 1865, 334 p. illus. by Hablot K. Browne.

Pub. also in Tauchnitz Collection of British authors, 1865, 3 vols., xviii, 1088 p.

Tr. into Danish: Kan du tilgive hende? 1866, 3 vols.

Tr. into Dutch: Kunt gij't haar vergeven? 1867, 3 vols.

Reviews

Muirhead, Finlay. England. (Blue guides). 2d ed, 1924, p. 444. "Near the foot of the lake (Hawes Water), is Thornthwaite, familiar to readers of Trollope's *Can you forgive her."*

Seccombe, Thomas, in Bookman (Lond.), June 1915, vol. 48, p. 65-69, 2 illus. by Hablot K. Browne, on pages 67 and 68.

These illustrations may have been meant for vol 2, but they were never used, as vol. 2 was illus. by Miss Taylor. The illus. are entitled "The Captain for the first time in his life tasted perfect bliss," and "The tramps."

Athenæum, Sept. 1865, no. 1975, p. 305-306.
Month, 1865, vol. 3, p. 319-323.
Nation (N. Y.), Sept. 28, 1865, vol. 1, p. 409-410.
Saturday review, Aug. 1865, vol. 20, p. 240-242.
Spectator, Sept. 2, 1865, vol. 38, p. 978-979.

Castle Richmond. In 3 vols. London, Chapman and Hall, 1860.

The ordinary First Edition has, at end of vol. 3 a 32-page publisher's catalogue, dated May 1860. It has been established that earlier copies were printed, presumably for foreign use, with a 16-page catalogue, dated February, 1860.

Pub. also in Tauchnitz Collection of British authors, 1860,
Pub. also by Harper, N. Y., 1860, 474 p.
2 vols., x, 704 p.

Tr. into Danish: Castle Richmond, fortælling, overs., 1860, 2 vols.

Tr. into Dutch: Het Kasteel Richmond, een verhaal tijdens den hongersnood in Ireland in 1846 en 1847, 1862, 2 vols, title vignette.

Tr. into French: Château-Richmond, tr. de l'anglais, 5 vols. 819 p. Naumberg, 1863. (Bibliothèque choisie.)

Tr. into German: Schloss Richmond, deutsch von A. Kretzschmar. 186-? 6 bde., 1085 p. (Bibliothek europäische)

Reviews

Baker, Ernest A., History in fiction, 1906, vol. 1, p. 167.
Brown, Stephen J., Ireland in fiction. New ed., 1919, p. 296.
Forgues, E. D., Romans de la vie anglaise: *The Bertrams* and *Castle Richmond,* in Revue des deux mondes, 1860, 2ᵉ pér., vol. 29, p. 369-398.
Thorold, Algar, Introduction, John Lane New Pocket edition of *Castle Richmond,* 1906.

Athenæum, May 1860, no. 1699, p. 681-682.
Harper's magazine, Aug. 1860, vol. 21, p. 410.
Saturday review, May 1860, vol. 9, p. 643-644.
Spectator, May 19, 1860, vol. 33, p. 477.

Christmas at Thompson Hall. In 1 vol. 91 p. illus., in Harper's half hour series, 1877, vol. 4.
Pub. also as the third story in *Why Frau Frohmann raised her prices, and other stories,* 1882.
Pub. also as the third story in *Frau Frohmann, and other stories,* 1882 (?), in Tauchnitz Collection of British authors.
Pub. separately with title: *Thompson Hall,* London, Sampson Low & Co., 1885, 127 p.
Tr. into German: Das Weihnachtsfest zu Thompsonhall, nacherzählt von Alice Salzbrunn (pseud.), in Familien bibliothek, 1891, no. 119.

Reviews

Harper's magazine, June 1877, vol. 55, p. 149.

The Claverings. In 2 vols. London, Smith, Elder and Co., 1867.
Sixteen illustrations by M. Ellen Edwards.
Appeared in Cornhill, Feb. 1866-May 1867, vol. 13-15.
Appeared also in Littell's, March 1866-Feb. 1867, vol. 88-92.
Appeared also in Galaxy, 1866-67, vol. 1-3, illustrated.
Pub. also by Harper, N. Y., 1866, 211 p.
Pub. also in Tauchnitz Collection of British authors, 1866, 2 vols, xii, 708 p.
Tr. into Dutch: De Claverings, uit het Eng. door J. C. v. Deventer, 1867, 2 vols., plate.
In Chapter II, we are told how Bishop Proudie, instructed by his wife, interfered with Rev. Mr. Clavering's hunting.

Reviews

Gorter, S., in De Gids, July, 1868, pt. III, p. 171-184.
Knight, J., in Fortnightly review, June 1867, vol. 7, p. 770-772.
Street, G. S., introduction to the Oxford university press edition (World's classics), 1924, p. v-xiv.

American Presbyterian and theological review, April 1867,
new ser., vol. 5, p. 346.
Athenæum, June 1867, no. 2068, p. 783.
Blackwood's magazine, Sept. 1867, vol. 102, p. 275-278.
    Same article in Littell's, Oct. 5, 1867, vol. 95, p. 16-18.
Harper's magazine, Dec. 1867, vol. 36, p. 128.
Saturday review, May 1867, vol. 23, p. 638-639.
    Same article in Littell's, June 22, 1867, vol. 93, p. 777-779.
Spectator, May 1867, vol. 40, p. 498-499.
    Same article in Littell's, June 22, 1867, vol. 93, p. 779-782.

Clergymen of the Church of England. In 1 vol., iv. 130 p.
London, Chapman and Hall, 1866.
    Reprinted from the Pall Mall gazette.

Reviews

Contemporary review, 1866, vol. 2, p. 240-262, Mr. Anthony
Trollope and the English clergy.

The commentaries of Cæsar. In 1 vol., vi, 182 p. London,
William Blackwood and Sons, 1870.
    In Blackwood's Ancient classics for English readers, no. 4.

Reviews

Athenæum, June 1870, no. 2224, p. 771.
Contemporary review, 1870, vol. 15, p. 314.
Dublin review, Jan. 1877, vol. 80, p. 127-141.
Spectator, June 1870, vol. 43, p. 757-758.

Cousin Henry. In 2 vols. London, Chapman and Hall, 1879.
    Pub. also by Harper, N. Y., 1879.
    Pub. also in Tauchnitz Collection of British authors,
1879, 280 p.
    Tr. into French: Le Cousin Henry, tr. de l'anglais par Mme.
Honorine Martel, 1882.

Reviews

Wallace, William, in Academy, Nov. 1879, vol. 16, p. 316.

Athenæum, Oct. 1879, no. 2712, p. 495.
Harper's magazine, Jan. 1880, vol. 60, p. 314.
Saturday review, Oct. 1879, vol. 48, p. 515-516.
Spectator, Oct. 18, 1879, vol. 52, p. 1319-1321.
Times (Lond.), Nov. 6, 1879, p. 6, col. 1.

Did he steal it? A comedy in three acts. 1869. Printed for
private circulation.
    "This is a dramatization of an episode in *The last chonicle
of Barset,* which Trollope prepared by special request, only to
have the play rejected by the commissioning manager."—
(From Sadleir's Excursions in Victorian bibliography, 1922,
p. 55.)

Doctor Thorne. In 3 vols. London, Chapman and Hall, 1858.
This is the third in the series *Barsetshire Novels.*
Pub. also by Harper, N. Y., 1858, 520 p.
Pub. also in Tauchnitz Collection of British authors,
1858, 2 vols., xii, 744 p.
Tr. into Danish: Doctor Thorne, fortælling, 1861, 3 vols.
Tr. into Dutch: De doctor, uit het Eng. door Mevr. van
Westerheene, 1860, 3 vols., illus.
Tr. into French: Le Docteur Thorne. 1863, 5 vols., 819 p.
(Bibliothèque choisie).
Tr. into French: Le Docteur Thorne, tr. de l'anglais par
deux collaborateurs de la "Revue britannique," 1864.
Tr. into German: Doctor Thorne, deutsch von A. Kretzsch-
mar, 186-? 6 bde., 1115 p. (in Bibliothek europäische).

Reviews

Montégut, Émile, Écrivains modernes de l'Angleterre, 1892,
vol. 3, p. 1-138, Anthony Trollope; p. 77-121, Le roman de
mœurs religieuses et aristocratiques, *Doctor Thorne.*
Newbolt, Sir Francis, Out of court, 1925, p. 73-82.
Osler, Sir William, in Harvey Cushing's Life of Sir
William Osler, 1925, vol. 2, p. 602 foot-note.
Sadleir, Michael, Trollope love story and Mary Thorne,
in Nineteenth century, Sept. 1924, vol. 96, 355-366.
Thorold, Algar, Introduction, John Lane New Pocket edi-
tion of *Doctor Thorne,* 1902.

Athenæum, June 1858, no. 1597, p. 719.
Harper's magazine, Sept. 1858, vol. 17, p. 693.
National review, Oct. 1858, vol. 7, p. 416-435.
North British review, June 1864, vol. 40, p. 369-401.
Saturday review, June 1858, vol. 5, p. 618-619.

Dr. Wortle's school. In 2 vols. London, Chapman and Hall,
1881.
Appeared anonymously in Blackwood's, May-Dec. 1880,
vol. 127-128.
Pub. also by Harper, N. Y., 1880.
Pub. also in Tauchnitz Collection of British authors, 1880,
286 p.
Tr. into Dutch: De school van Dr. Wortle, 1881.

Reviews

Athenæum, Jan. 1881, no. 2777, p. 93.
Critic (N. Y.), Feb. 12, 1881, vol. 1, p. 35.
Harper's magazine, May 1881, vol. 62, p. 636.
Nation (N. Y.), March 10, 1881, vol. 32, p. 172-173.
Saturday review, Jan. 1881, vol. 51, p. 121-122.
Times (Lond.), April 16, 1881, p. 10, col. 3.
Westminster review, July 1881, new ser., vol. 60, p. 283-284.

The Duke's children. In 3 vols. London, Chapman and Hall, 1880.
> This is the sixth in the series *Parliamentary Novels*.
> Pub. also by Harper, N. Y., 1880.
> Pub. also in Tauchnitz Collection of British authors, 1880, 3 vols.

Reviews

Sedgwick, A. G., in Nation (N. Y.), Aug. 1880, vol. 31, p. 138-139.

Athenæum, May 1880, no. 2744, p. 694-695.
Harper's magazine, Sept. 1880, vol. 61, p. 643.
Saturday review, June 12, 1880, vol. 49, p. 767-768.
Spectator, June 12, 1880, vol. 53, p. 754-755.
Westminster review, Oct. 1880, new ser., vol. 58, p. 574.

The Eustace diamonds. In 3 vols. London, Chapman and Hall, 1873.
> This is the third in the series *Parliamentary Novels*.
> Appeared in Fortnightly review, July 1871-Feb. 1873, vols. 16-19.
> Appeared also in Galaxy, Sept. 1871-Jan. 1873, vols. 12-15.
> Pub. also in Asher's Collection of English authors, 1873, 2 vols.
> Pub. also by Harper, N. Y., in 1872, 351 p. and in 1873, 351 p.
> Tr. into Dutch: De diamanten der familie Eustace, uit het Eng. door J. W. Straatman, 1873-75, 3 vols.

Reviews

Athenæum, Oct. 1872, no. 2348, p. 527-528.
Harper's magazine, Dec. 1872, vol. 46, p. 140.
Nation (N. Y.), Nov. 14, 1872, vol. 15, p. 319-320.
Saturday review, Nov. 1872, vol. 34, p. 637-638.
Spectator, Oct. 26, 1872, vol. 46, p. 1365-1366.
Times (Lond.), Oct. 30, 1872, p. 1, col. 2.

An eye for an eye. In 2 vols. London, Chapman and Hall, 1879. (Written in 1871-72.)
> Pub. also by Harper, N. Y., 1879, 35 p.
> Pub. also in Tauchnitz Collection of British authors, 1879, 295 p.
> Tr. into French: Œil pour œil, tr. de l'anglais par Amy Davy, 1880.
> Tr. into Hungarian: Szemet-szemért, regény, angolból ford. Huszár Imre, Budapest, 1875, 435 p.

Reviews

Lasselle, S. C., Morality in authorship, in The Author (Boston), 1889, vol. 1, p. 82.
Littledale, R. F., in Academy, Feb. 1879, vol. 15, p. 117.

Athenæum, Jan. 1879, no. 2672, p. 47.
Nation (N. Y.), April 24, 1879, vol. 28, p. 290.
Saturday review, March 1879, vol. 47, p. 410-411.
Spectator, Feb. 15, 1879, vol. 52, p. 210-211.

The fixed period. In 2 vols. Edin. and London, Wm. Black-
wood and Sons, 1882.
A story of the year 1980.
Appeared anonymously in Blackwood's, Oct. 1881-Mar. 1882,
vol. 130-132.
Pub. also by Harper, N. Y., 1882.
Pub. also in Tauchnitz Collection of British authors, 1882,
280 p.

Reviews

Bradford, Gamaliel, Trollope and the Osler treatment, in
Nation (N. Y.), June 8, 1905, vol. 80, p. 458.
Church, James Robb, Sir William Osler and the fixed
period, in Military surgeon, 1920, vol. 46, p. xlvi, 678-682.
Cushing, Harvey, Life of Sir William Osler, 1925, vol. I,
p. 664-672, including an extract by Basil Lanneau Gildersleeve
on the *"Fixed period* episode," on page 671.
Mackall, Leonard L., Sir William Osler, in Papers of the
Bibliographical society of America, 1919, vol. 14, p. 20-23.
      (Same article, in part only, in Tribune (N. Y.), Sunday
      Book section, Sept. 21, 1924, p. 23.)
Osler, Sir William, Aequanimitas, 2d. ed., 1910, pref. p. viii,
and p. 389-411, Fixed period.
———————— Valedictory address at Johns Hopkins uni-
versity, Feb. 22, 1905, in Journal of the American medical
association, March 4, 1905, vol. 44, p. 705-710.
Powell, Lyman P., William Osler and old age, in Times
(N. Y.), Jan. 4, 1920, Sunday, Section 8, p. 18.
Willey, Day Allen, "Osler," in Critic (N. Y.), May 1905,
vol. 46, p. 411-415.
Williams G. Huntington, Osler and the *"Fixed period,"*
Toronto, 1926, 8 p. (From a Bibliography in "Appreciations
and reminiscences of Sir William Osler" pub. in Montreal, 1926,
p. 626.)

Athenæum, March 1882, no. 2837, p. 314-315.
Harper's magazine, June 1882, vol. 65, p. 156.
———————— June 1905, vol. 111, Editor's easy chair,
p, 147-150.
Nation (N. Y.), May 4, 1882, vol. 34, p. 385.
Saturday review, April 1882, vol. 53, p. 434-435.
Spectator, March 18, 1882, vol. 55, p. 360-361.
———————— March 4, 1905, p. 318-319, The power of old
age.
Times (Lond.), April 12, 1882, p. 3, col. 6.

Tribune (N. Y.), Feb. 25, 1905, p. 9, col. 1, Dr. Osler meant it.

Westminster review, July 1882, new ser., vol. 62, p. 285-286.

Framley Parsonage. In 3 vols. London, Smith, Elder and Co., 1861.

Six illustrations by J. E. Millais.

This is the fourth in the series *Barsetshire Novels.*

Appeared anonymously in Cornhill, Jan. 1860-April 1861, vols. 1-3.

Pub. also by Harper, N. Y., 1861, 530 p., 6 illus.

Pub. also in Tauchnitz Collection of British authors, 1861, 2 vols., x, 725 p.

Tr. into German: Das Pfarrhaus Framley, deutsch von A. Kretzchmar, 6 bde., 1064 p., 1. aufl., 1864; 2. aufl. 1867.

Reviews

Thorold, Algar, Introduction, John Lane New Pocket edition of *Framley Parsonage,* 1903.

American theological review, Oct. 1861, vol. 3, p. 765.

Athenæum, April 1861, no. 1747, i, p. 528.

Dublin university magazine, April 1862, v. 59, p. 405-406.

Harper's magazine, Sept. 1861, vol. 23, p. 548.

———— ———— Nov. 1879, vol. 59, p. 956.

North British review, June 1864, vol. 40, p. 369-401.

Saturday review, May 1861, vol. 11, p. 451-452.

The Golden Lion of Granpere. In 1 vol., 353 p., London, Tinsley Brothers, 1872.

Appeared in Harper's magazine, Feb.-Sept. 1872, vol. 44-45, 24 illustrations.

Appeared also in Good words, vol. for 1872, 24 illus.

Pub. also by Harper, N. Y., 1872, 124 p., 13 illus., 8 plates.

Pub. also in Tauchnitz Collection of British authors, 1872, 312 p.

Tr. into Dutch: Het Hôtel de Gouden Leeuw, naar het Eng. door Mw. v. Westrheene, 1872.

Tr. into German: Der Goldene Löwe in Grenpere (Elsass), aus dem englischen von Lina Kayser, Leipzig, 1873, 316 p.

Reviews

Walpole, Hugh, Introduction to *Golden Lion of Granpere,* 1925, p. vii-ix (Everyman's edition).

Athenæum, May 1872, no. 2326, p. 651-653.

Harper's magazine, Sept. 1872, vol. 45, p. 624.

Nation (N. Y.), Aug. 22, 1872, vol. 15, p. 126.

Old and new, Sept. 1872, vol. 6, p. 352.

Saturday review, June 1872, vol. 33, p. 833-835.

Spectator, May 18, 1872, vol. 45, p. 630-631.

Harry Heathcote of Gangoil. In 1 vol., 313 p., London, Sampson Low, Marston Low and Searle, 1874.

Appeared in London Graphic, Christmas number, Dec. 25, 1873, vol. 8, p. 1-23, 6 plates.

Appeared also in Littell's, Jan. 24-Mar. 7, 1874, vol. 120.

Pub. also by Harper, N. Y., 1874, 61 p.

Pub. also in Tauchnitz Collection of British authors, 1874, 232 p.

Reviews

Owen, F. M., in Academy, April 1875, vol. 7, p. 396.

Saintsbury, George, in Academy, Dec. 1874, vol. 6, p. 652.

Athenæum, Nov. 1874, no. 2454, p. 606.

Harper's magazine, April 1874, vol. 48, p. 747.

Saturday review, Nov. 1874, vol. 38, p. 609-610.

Spectator, Feb. 1875, vol. 48, p. 247-248.

Westminster review, April 1875, new ser., vol. 47, p. 558.

He knew he was right. In 2 vols. London, Strahan and Company, 1869.

Sixty-four illustrations by Marcus Stone.

Appeared in Every Saturday, Oct. 1868-May 1869, vol. 6-7.

Pub. also by Harper, N. Y., 1870, 335 p.

Pub. also in Tauchnitz Collection of British authors, 1870, 3 vols.

Tr. into Dutch: Wie heeft gelijk? uit het Eng. door J. C. van Deventer, 1870, 3 vols, 3 plates.

Reviews

Hawk, Affable, in New statesman, April 22, 1922, vol. 19, p. 67.

Harper's magazine, May 1869, vol. 38, p. 854.

Public opinion (Lond.), June 12, 1869, vol. 15, p. 744.

——— ——— July 3, 1869, vol. 16, p. 13.

Saturday review, June 1869, vol. 27, p. 751-753.

Spectator, June 1869, vol. 42, p. 706-708.

Times (Lond.), Aug. 28, 1869, p. 4, col. 1.

How the "Mastiffs" went to Iceland. In 1 vol., 46 p., London, Virtue and Co., 1878.

Issued for private circulation only, in quarto form.

Illustrations by Mrs. Hugh Blackburn, col. map, 14 pencil drawings, 2 photographs.

In six of these drawings, Trollope figures prominently. He is represented also in one of the photographs, but very indistinctly.

Appeared in Fortnightly review, Aug. 1878, vol. 30, p. 175-190, under the title: *Iceland.*

Hunting sketches. In 1 vol., iv, 115 p., London, Chapman and Hall, 1865.
Reprinted from the Pall Mall gazette.

Reviews

Stewart, Charles, in Fortnightly review, 1865, vol. 1, p. 765-767.

London Reader, 26 Aug. 1865, vol. 6, p. 233.
Spectator, May 27, 1865, vol. 38, p. 587-588.

Is he Popenjoy? In 3 vols. London, Chapman and Hall, 1878.
Appeared in All the year round, 1877.
Pub. also by Harper, N. Y., 1878.
Pub. also in Tauchnitz Collection of British authors, 1878, 3 vols.
Tr. into German: Ist er Popenjoy? 1878. 3 bde. (Britannia-bibliothek, Strassburg).

Reviews

Littledale, R. F., in Academy, June 1878, vol. 13, p. 505.

Athenæum, May 1878, no. 2636, p. 567.
Harper's magazine, Aug. 1878, vol. 57, p. 468.
Saturday review, June 1878, vol. 45, p. 695-696.
Spectator, Oct. 1878, vol. 51, p. 1243-1244.
Times (Lond.), Sept. 14, 1878, p. 4, col. 6.

John Caldigate. In 3 vols. London, Chapman and Hall, 1879.
Appeared in Blackwood's, April, 1878-June, 1879, vol. 123-125.
Pub. also by Harper, N. Y., 1879.
Pub. also in Tauchnitz Collection of British authors, 1879, 3 vols.

Reviews

Purcell, E. in Academy, July 1879, vol. 16, p. 4-5.

Athenæum, June 1879, no. 2694, p. 755.
Harper's magazine, Sept. 1879, vol. 59, p. 631.
Saturday review, Aug. 1879, vol. 48, p. 216-217.
Spectator, 1879, July 19, vol. 52, p. 916-917.
Times (Lond.), Aug. 8, 1879, p. 3, col. 4.

The Kellys and the O'Kellys. In 3 vols. London, Henry Colburn, 1848.
Pub. also by Harper, N. Y., 1848.
Note.—Lord Ballandine and Fannie Wyndham, the hero and heroine, who have been estranged before the story begins, do not meet again until the middle of the next to the

last chapter,—and their only recorded conversation is the two exclamations there set down:—"My own Fanny!—once more my own!" "Oh, Frank! dear Frank!"

Reviews

Brown, Stephen J., Ireland in fiction, New ed., 1919, p. 296.

Athenæum, July 1848, no. 1081, p. 701.

Kept in the dark. In 2 vols. London, Chatto and Windus, 1882.
 Frontispiece by J. E. Millais.
 Appeared in Good words, vol. for 1882 (8 installments), 1 plate.
 Pub. also by Harper, N. Y., 1882.
 Pub. also in Tauchnitz Collection of British authors, 1882, 288 p.
 Tr. into Dutch: In het duister gelaten, naar het Eng., 1883.

Reviews

Academy, Nov. 1882, vol. 22, p. 377-378.
Athenæum, Nov. 1882, no. 2873, p. 658.
Graphic (Lond.), Dec. 23, 1882, vol. 26, p. 710, col. 2.
Harper's magazine, Jan. 1883, vol. 66, p. 317.
Nation (N. Y.), Nov. 23, 1882, vol. 35, p. 447-448.
Spectator, Jan. 1883, vol. 56, p. 88-89.
Westminster review, Jan. 1883, new ser., vol. 63, p. 287.

Lady Anna. In 2 vols. London, Chapman and Hall, 1874.
 Appeared in Fortnightly, April, 1873-April, 1874, vol. 19-21 (new ser., v. 13-15).
 Pub also by Harper, N. Y., 1874, 125 p.
 Pub. also in Tauchnitz Collection of British authors, 1873, 2 vols.

Reviews

Saintsbury, George, in Academy, May 1874, vol. 5, p. 482-483.

Harper's magazine, July 1874, vol. 49, p. 290.
Nation (N. Y.), July 2, 1874, vol. 19, p. 9-11.
Saturday review, May 1874, vol. 37, p. 598-599.
Times (Lond.), June 24, 1874, p. 5, col. 1.

The Lady of Launay. In 1 vol., 125 p., in Harper's half hour series, 1878, vol. 74.
 Pub. also as the second story in *Why Frau Frohmann raised her prices, and other stories,* 1882.

The landleaguers. In 3 vols. London, Chatto and Windus, 1883.

Unfinished. "This novel was to have contained sixty chapters. Trollope had not finished the forty-ninth."
"Appeared also in a weekly paper called 'Life' in the autumn of 1882." (Authority, Miss Lavington's Bibliography in T. H. S. Escott's Anthony Trollope, 1913).
Pub. also by Harper, N. Y., 1883.
Tr. into Dutch: De land-ligers, naar het Eng. vert. door A. A. Deenik, 1885, 2 vols.

Reviews

Brown, Stephen J., Ireland in fiction, New ed., 1919, p. 296-297.
Purcell, E., in Academy, Nov. 1883, vol. 24, p. 327-328.

Athenæum, Nov. 1883, no. 2926, p. 665-666.
Continent, Nov. 1882, vol. 2, p. 605.
———————— Dec. 1883, vol. 4, p. 702.
Spectator, Dec. 1883, vol. 56, p. 1627.
Westminster review, Jan. 1884, vol. 121 (new. ser., vol. 65), p. 276-277.

The last chronicle of Barset. In 2 vols. London, Smith, Elder and Co., 1867.
Thirty-two illustrations by George H. Thomas, also many chapters have vignette head pieces.
This is the sixth in the series *Barsetshire Novels*.
Pub. also by Harper, N. Y., 1866.
Pub. also in Tauchnitz Collection of British authors, 1866, 3 vols., 1197 p.
Tr. into Dutch: De verloren wissel, naar het Eng. 1869. 3 vols. 3 plates.
Two extracts appear in Sir Arthur Quiller-Couch's Oxford book of English prose, 1925, p. 742-749.

Reviews

Grierson, Herbert J. C., in his preface (p. iv-v) to Yü Hsiu Sen's Ancient Chinese parables, 1924.
Howells, W. D., in Harper's bazar, June 1901, vol. 35, p. 102-109, 1 illus.

Athenæum, Aug. 1867, no. 2075, p. 141.
Blackwood's, Sept. 1867, vol. 102, p. 275-278.
Harper's magazine, Dec. 1867, vol. 36, p. 128.
Notes and queries, June 24, 1916, series 12, vol. 1, p. 507, An inconsistency in the *Last Chronicle*.
Spectator, July 13, 1867, vol. 40, p. 778-780.

The life of Cicero. In 2 vols. London, Chapman and Hall, 1880.
Pub. also by Harper, N. Y., 1881, 2 vols.

Reviews

Fowler, W. W., in Academy, Jan. 1881, vol. 19, p. 91-92.
Jeans, G. E., *Life and letters of Cicero,* 1891, p. 404.
Stevenson, Robert Louis. Works. New York, Scribner, 1898,
vol. 22, Letters and miscellanies, p. 249.
> Reprinted from Contemporary review, April 1885, vol. 47,
> p. 552.
> The same quoted in Lane Cooper's Theories of style,
> 1923, p. 371.

Athenæum, Aug. 1881, no. 2806, p. 170-172.
Blackwood's, Feb, 1881, vol. 129, p. 211-228.
Critic (N. Y.), Jan. 29, 1881, vol. 1, p. 3-4.
Harper's magazine, April 1881, vol. 62, p. 791.
Nation (N. Y.), July 28, 1881, vol. 33, p. 75-76.
Saturday review, Feb. 1881, vol. 51, p. 279-280.
Spectator, March 1881, vol. 54, p. 353-354.
Springfield (Mass.) Republican, March 22, 1881, Books, au-
thors and art.
Westminster review, April 1881, new ser., vol. 59, p. 605-606.

Linda Tressel. In 2 vols. Edin. and London, Wm. Blackwood and Sons, 1868.
> Published anonymously.
> Appeared anonymously in Blackwood's, 1867-68, vol. 102-
> 103.
> Appeared also in Littell's, 1867-68, vol. 95-97.
> Pub. also by Harper, N. Y., 1868.

Reviews

Courtney, William Prideaux, The secrets of our national
literature, 1908, p. 98-99.
Fry, Henry Walter. In Times (N. Y.), Sunday, June 12,
1921, Section VII, p. 12, col. 2. Trollope's novels.

Littell's, July 1868, vol. 98, p. 128 ("From London review").
Nation (N. Y.), June 18, 1868, vol. 6, p. 494-495.
Spectator, May 9, 1868, vol. 41, p. 562-563.

Lord Palmerston (English political leaders). In 1 vol., 220 p.
London, Wm. Isbister, 1882.

Reviews

Academy, Aug. 1882, vol. 22, p. 98-99.
Athenæum, Sept. 1882, no. 2864, p. 367.
Nation (N. Y.), Feb. 1883, vol. 36, p. 128-130.
Saturday review, Aug. 1882, vol. 54, p. 182-183.
Westminster review, Oct. 1882, new ser., vol. 62, p. 566

The Macdermots of Ballycloran. In 3 vols. London, Thomas Cautley Newby, 1847.
> This was Trollope's first novel.
> Pub. also by Harper, N. Y., 1847.

Reviews

Brown, Stephen J., Ireland in fiction, New ed., 1919, p. 296.
Thorold, Algar, Introduction, John Lane New Pocket edition of *The Macdermots,* 1906.

Athenæum, May 1847, no. 1020, p. 517.
North British review, June 1864, vol. 40, p. 369-401.

Marion Fay. In 3 vols. London, Chapman and Hall, 1882.
> Appeared in London Graphic, Dec. 31, 1881-June 3, 1882, vol. 24-25, 26 illus. by W. Small.
> Pub. also by Harper, N. Y., 1882, 119 p., 27 illus. by W. Small. One of the illus. is given twice.
> Pub. also in Tauchnitz Collection of British authors, 1882, 2 vols.
> Tr. into Norwegian: Marion Fay; eller, Den dødsdømte, oversat fra det engelske af W. S. Juell, 1883, 2 vols., 8 illus.

Reviews

Athenæum, June 1882, no. 2852, p. 793-794.
Critic (N. Y.), July 29, 1882, vol. 2, p. 201.
Harper's magazine, Aug. 1882, vol. 65, p. 478.
Nation (N. Y.), July 27, 1882, vol. 35, p. 78-79.
Saturday review, July 1882, vol. 54, p. 64-65.
Spectator, Aug. 19, 1882, vol. 55, p. 1088-1089.

Miss Mackenzie. In 2 vols. London, Chapman and Hall, 1865.
> Pub. also by Harper, N. Y., 1865, 139 p.
> Pub. also in Asher's Collection of English authors, 1876, 2 vols.
> Pub. also in Asher's Continental library, 1880, 2 vols.
> Tr. into Dutch: Miss Mackenzie, uit het Eng. vert. door J. H. Ebbeler, 1876, 2 vols.
> Several of the characters appear also in *The Bertrams,* in the *Parliamentary novels,* and (the lawyers) in *The way we live now.*

Reviews

Dublin university magazine, May 1865, vol. 65, p. 576.
Nation (N. Y.), July 13, 1865, vol. 1, p. 51-52.
Reader (London), 1865, vol. 7, p. 596.
Saturday review, March 4, 1865, vol. 19, p. 263-265.
Spectator, March 4, 1865, vol. 38, p. 244-245.
Times (Lond.), 23 Aug. 1865, p. 12, col. 1.

Mr. Scarborough's family. In 3 vols. London, Chatto and Windus, 1883.
Appeared in All the year round, May 27, 1882-June 16, 1883, vol. 29-32.
Pub. also in Asher's Collection of English authors, 1883, 3 vols.
Pub. also by Harper, N. Y., 1883.
Pub also by Lovell, N. Y., 1883, 488 p.

Reviews

Wallace, William, in Academy, May 1883, vol. 23, p. 344.

Athenæum, May 1883, no. 2898, p. 600.
Harper's magazine, Aug. 1883, vol. 67, p. 479.
Nation (N. Y.), June 28, 1883, vol. 36, p. 552-553.
Saturday review, May 1883, vol. 55, p. 642-643.
Spectator, May 1883, vol. 56, p. 612-613.
Westminster review, July 1883, new ser., vol. 64, p. 301.

New South Wales and Queensland. In 1 vol., 209 p. London, Chapman and Hall, 1874.
Separate issue of Part 1 of Trollope's *Australia and New Zealand,* 1873, which see.

New Zealand. In 1 vol., 166 p., map. London, Chapman and Hall, 1874.
Separate issue of Part 3 of Trollope's *Australia and New Zealand,* 1873, which see.

Nina Balatha. In 2 vols. Edin. and London. Wm. Blackwood and Sons, 1867.
Published anonymously.
Appeared anonymously in Blackwood's, 1867-68, vol. 100-101.
Appeared also in Littell's, Oct. 13, 1866-Feb. 9, 1867, vol. 91-92.
Pub. also by Harper, N. Y., 1867.
Pub. also in Tauchnitz Collection of British authors, 1867. 312 p.

Reviews

Courtney, William Prideaux, The secrets of our national literature, 1908, p. 98-99.
Fry, Henry Walter, in Times (N. Y.), Sunday, June 12, 1921, Section VII, p. 12, col. 2. Trollope's novels.

Athenæum, March 1867, no. 2053, p. 288.
Littell's, July 11, 1868, vol. 98, p. 128 ("From London Review").
Spectator, March 23, 1867, vol. 40, p. 329-330.

The noble jilt: a comedy, ed. with a preface by Michael Sadleir. In 1 vol., xix, 181 p. London, Constable and Company, 1923.

Written in 1850, now printed for the first time. Bound uniformly with the first edition of *Can you forgive her?* "This edition is limited to 500 copies."

Review

Christian science monitor, Aug. 29, 1923, p. 14 (with portrait), signed, E. F. H.

North America. In 2 vols. Folded map. London, Chapman and Hall, 1862.

Pub. also by Harper, N. Y., in 1862 and in 1863, vii, 623 p.
Pub. also in Tauchnitz Collection of British authors, 1862, 3 vols, xviii, 981 p.
Tr. into German: Nord-Amerika, deutsch von A. Diezmann, 1862, 3 bde., xxiv, 938 p.

Reviews

Brooks, John Graham, As others see us, 1910, p. 48 footnote, 78 foot-note, 207-208.

Cooke, J. R., in North American review, Oct. 1862, vol. 95, p. 416-436.

Hardman, Sir William, A mid-Victorian Pepys, 1923, p. 159-160.

Nevins, Allan. American social history as recorded by British travellers, 1923, p. 301-307, 406-421.

Rhodes, James Ford, History of the civil war, 1917, p. 278.
——— ——— History of the United States, 1919, vol. 3, p. 518 and 579.
——— ——— Lectures on the American Civil War, 1913, p. 108.

Tuckerman, Henry T., America and her commentators, 1864, p. 232-244.

American theological review, July 1882, vol. 4, p. 581-582.
Athenæum, May 1862, no. 1804, p. 685-687.
Blackwood's, Sept. 1862, vol. 92, p. 372-390.
Chamber's journal, June 28, 1862, ser. 3, vol. 17, p. 408-409, Anthony Trollope on the United States.
Dublin university magazine, July 1862, vol. 60, p. 75-82.
Fraser's magazine, Aug. 1862, vol. 66, p. 256-264.
Harper's magazine, July 1862, vol. 25, p. 262-263.
Quarterly review (London), Oct. 1862, vol. 112, p. 535-570.
——— ——— April 1864, vol. 115, p. 291.
Presbyterian quarterly review, July 1862, vol. 11, p. 173.
Saturday review, May 1862, vol. 13, p. 625-626.
Times (Lond.), June 11, 1862, p. 6.

An old man's love. In 2 vols. Edin. and London, Wm. Blackwood and Sons, 1884.

Trollope had completed this novel, but it was not published until after his death.

Pub. also by Harper, N. Y., 1884.

Pub. also by Lovell, N. Y., 1884, 176 p.

Pub. also in Tauchnitz Collection of British authors, 1884, 278 p.

Tr. into Dutch: De liefde van een ouden vrijer, naar het Eng., 1885.

Reviews

Dawkins, C. E., in Academy, March 1884, p. 220.

Wedgwood, Julia, in Contemporary review, July 1884, vol. 46, p. 149-151.

Athenæum, April 1884, no. 2945, p. 438.

Harper's magazine, July 1884, vol. 69, p. 318.

Saturday review, March 1884, vol. 57, p. 414-415.

Times (Lond.), April 14, 1884, p. 3, col. 3.

Westminster review, July 1884, vol. 122, p. 305.

Orley Farm. In 2 vols. London, Chapman and Hall, 1862. Forty illustrations by J. E. Millais.

Appeared in Harper's monthly, May, 1861-Dec. 1862, vol. 22-26, 40 illus.

Pub. also by Harper, N. Y., 1862, 338 p., 38 illus.

Pub. also in Tauchnitz Collection of British authors, 1862, 3 vols., xvii, 1068 p.

Tr. into Dutch: De aanklagt van meineed, naar het Eng. 1864. 2 vols. 2 title vignettes.

Tr. into German: Orley Farm, deutsch von A. Kretzschmar, 186-? 5 bde., 1053 p.

Tr. into German: Orley-Farm, aus dem engl. von Clara Markgraff, 1865, 6 bde., 1244 p.

Reviews

Newbolt, Sir Francis, Reg. *v.* Mason, in Nineteenth century, Feb. 1924, vol. 95, p. 227-236.

———— ———— Out of court, 1925, p. 7-73.

Thorold, Algar, Introduction, John Lane New Pocket edition of *Orley Farm,* 1906.

American Presbyterian theological review, April 1863, new ser., vol. 1, p. 361.

Athenæum, March 1861, no. 1741, p. 319-320.

———— ———— Oct. 1862, no. 1823, p. 425-426.

Cornhill, Nov. 1862, vol. 6, p. 702-704.

Dublin university magazine, April 1863, vol. 61, p. 437.

Harper's magazine, April 1863, vol. 26, p. 704.

National review, Jan. 1863, vol. 16, p. 27-40.
North British review, June 1864, vol. 40, p. 369-401.
Saturday review, Oct. 1862, vol. 14, p. 444-445.
Spectator, Oct. 11, 1862, vol. 35, p. 1136-1138.
Times (Lond.), Dec. 26, 1862, p. 5, col. 4.

Phineas, Finn. In 2 vols. London, Virtue and co., 1869.
20 illustrations by J. E. Millais.
This is the second in the series *Parliamentary Novels.*
Appeared in St. Paul's magazine, Oct. 1867-May 1869, vol.
1-4, illus.
Appeared also in Littell's, Nov. 1867-April 1869, vols. 95-
101.
Pub. also by Harper, N. Y., 1868, 235 p., 17 illus.
Pub. also in Tauchnitz Collection of British authors, 1868,
3 vols.
Tr. into Dutch: Phineas Finn, een verkiezingsroman met
een woord tot inleiding van J. H. Maronier, 1870, 3 vols., 3
plates.

Reviews

Brown, Stephen J., Ireland in fiction, New ed., 1919, p. 296.
Harrison, Frederic, Critical introduction to *Phineas Finn,*
London, Bell, 1911, 2 vols.

Contemporary review, 1869, vol. 12, p. 142-143 (signed:
M. B.).
Dublin review, 1869, vol. 65, (new ser., vol. 13), p. 361-377.
De Gids, Dec. 1870, pt. IV, p. 546-547.
Harper's magazine, May 1869, vol. 38, p. 854.
Notes and queries, Nov. 2, 1907, 10th series, vol. 8, p. 349,
Key to the political characters in *Phineas Finn* (signed:
W. B. H.).
Saturday review, March 1869, vol. 27, p. 431-432.
Spectator, March 20, 1869, vol. 42, p. 356-357.
———————— Jan. 3, 1874, vol. 47, p. 9-10, *Phineas Finn* in
America and England.
———————— May 3, 1913, vol. 110, p. 746-747, A political
novel.
Same article in Littell's, June 14, 1913, vol. 277, p. 691-
694.
Times (London), Literary supplement, Nov. 9, 1911, p. 437-
438, 3 col.
Same article in Littell's, Dec. 16, 1911, vol. 271, p. 683-
687, A political novel.

Phineas, Redux. In 2 vols. London, Chapman and Hall,
1874.
Twenty-four illustrations by Frank Hall.
This is the fourth in the series *Parliamentary Novels.*

Appeared in London Graphic, July 19, 1873-Jan. 10, 1874,
vol. 8-9, 24 illus.
Pub. also by Harper, N. Y., 1874, 255 p., 24 illus.
Pub. also in Asher's Collection of English authors, 1874,
3 vols.

Reviews

Brown, Stephen J., Ireland in fiction, New ed., 1919, p. 296.
Dicey, A V., in Nation (N. Y.), 1874, vol. 18, p. 174-175.
Simcox, Edith, in Academy, Feb. 1874, vol. 5, p. 141-143.

Athenæum, Jan. 1874, no. 2411, p. 53.
Harper's magazine, June 1874, vol. 49, p. 135.
Saturday review, Feb. 1874, vol. 37, p. 186-187.
Spectator, Jan. 3, 1874, vol. 47. p. 15-17.
————————— May 3, 1913, vol. 110, p. 746-747, A political
novel.
    Same article in Littell's, June 14, 1913, vol. 277, p. 691-694.
    Times (Lond.), Literary supplement, Nov. 9, 1911, p. 437-
438, 3 col.
    Same article in Littell's, Dec. 16, 1911, vol. 271, p. 683-
687, A political novel.

The Prime minister. In 4 vols. London, Chapman and Hall,
1876.
    This is the fifth in the series *Parliamentary Novels.*
    Pub. also by Harper, N. Y., 1876, 252 p.
    Pub. also in Tauchnitz Collection of British authors, 1876,
4 vols.

Reviews

Littledale, R. F., in Academy, July 1876, vol. 10, p. 106-107.

Athenæum, Dec. 1875, no. 2512, p. 829.
————————— July 1876, no. 2540, p. 14-15.
Harper's magazine, Aug. 1876, vol. 53, p. 467-468.
Nation (N. Y.), July 20, 1876, vol. 23, p. 45-46.
Saturday review, Oct. 1876, vol. 42, p. 481-482.
Spectator, July 22, 1876, vol. 49, p. 922-923.
Times (Lond.), Aug. 18, 1876, p. 4, col. 4.

Rachel, Ray. In 2 vols. London, Chapman and Hall, 1863.
    "A later and cheaper edition contained one illustration by
Millais."—Authority, Margaret Lavington, in T. H. S. Escott's
Anthony Trollope, 1913.
    George H. Sargent says, in Boston evening transcript,
Dec. 11, 1912: "Date usually given as 1863, but there is a
copy in the British Museum dated 1862."
    Mr. Michael Sadleir writes, Nov. 1925 (in re Sargent's
note), that there never was such a copy in the British Museum Library, and that the error in their Catalogue to that
effect has now been corrected to 1863.

Pub. also by Harper, N. Y., 1863.
Pub. also in Tauchnitz Collections of British authors, 1863, 2 vols., x, 556 p.
Tr. into French: Rachel Ray, tr. de l'anglais par L. Martel, 1889, 2 vols.

Reviews

Thorold, Algar, Introduction, John Lane New Pocket edition of *Rachel Ray,* 1906.

American Presbyterian and theological review, Jan. 1864, new ser., vol. 2, p. 185.
Athenæum, Oct. 1863, no. 1877, p. 492-494.
Good words, 1884, p. 248-252, port.
Harper's magazine, Jan. 1864, vol. 28, p. 274.
London Reader, 17 Oct. 1863, vol. 2, p. 437-438 (signed: E. D.).
Saturday review, Oct. 1863, vol. 16, p. 554-555.
Times (Lond.), Dec. 25, 1863, p. 4, col. 3.

Ralph the heir. In 3 vols. London, Hurst and Blackett, 1871.
Re-issued in the same year. In 1 vol., iv, 434 p., 18 illustrations by F. A. Fraser, London, Strahan and Co., 1871.
Appeared in St. Paul's magazine, Supplements, Jan. 1870-July 1871. 11 illus.
Appeared also in Appleton's journal, Supplements, Feb. 12, 1870-May 27, 1871, vol. 3-5, 13 illus.
Pub. also by Harper (N. Y.), 1871, iv, 282 p., 18 illus.
Pub. also in Tauchnitz Collection of British authors, 1871, 2 vols.
Tr. into Danish: Arvingen Ralph, 1872, 2 vols.
Tr. into Swedish: Ralph, öfv., 1874, 2 vols.

Reviews

Bristed, C. A., in North American review, April 1871, vol. 112, p. 433-441.
Walker, Hugh, The literature of the Victorian era, 1913, p. 759.

Athenæum, April 1871, no. 2268, p. 456.
Graphic, May 6, 1871, vol. 3, p. 418.
Harper's magazine, Aug. 1871, vol. 43, p. 458.
Saturday review, April 1871, vol. 31, p. 437-438.
Spectator, April 1871, vol. 44, p. 450-452.
Times (London), April 17, 1871, p. 6, col. 1.

The revolt of man, 1882.
This work of Sir Walter Besant's (the 1st ed. anonymous), was attributed to Anthony Trollope, also to Charles Dilke (see Westminster review, July, 1882, new ser., vol. 62, p. 285).

Saint Paul's. A monthly magazine, edited by Anthony Trollope, London, Virtue and Co., 1868-74.
> With later nos., publishers changed to Strahan & Co., and Henry S. King & Co.
> First no. is Oct. 1867, vol. 1, no. 1. Last no. is March 1874, vol. 14, no. 3.

Reviews

Nicoll, Sir William Robertson, Dicken's own story, 1923, p. 186.
Oliphant, Mrs. M. O. W., The Victorian age of English literature, 1892, vol. 2, p. 306.

Spectator, Oct. 1867, vol. 40, p. 1120-1121, Mr. Trollope's new magazine.

Sir Harry Hotspur of Humblethwaite. In 1 vol. vii, 323 p. London, Hurst and Blackett, 1871.
> Appeared in Macmillan's, May-Dec. 1870, v. 22-23.
> Pub. also by Harper, N. Y., 1871, 112 p.
> Pub. also in Tauchnitz Collection of British authors, 1871, 310 p.
> A new edition pub. by Macmillan and Co., London and New York, 1871.
> Tr. into Dutch: Emily Hotspur; of, Hoe een meisje kan liefhebben, naar het Eng. door S. J. Andriessen, 1871.

Reviews

Heijse, J. H. C., in De Gids, Jan. 1873, pt. 1, p. 181-188.

Athenæum, Nov. 1870, no. 2247, p. 654.
Harper's magazine, April 1871, vol. 42, p. 779-780.
Saturday review, July 2, 1870, vol. 30, p. 753-755.
Spectator, Nov. 1870, vol. 43, p. 1415-1416.
Times (Lond.), Nov. 16, 1870, p. 4, col. 1.

The Small House at Allington. In 2 vols. London, Smith, Elder and Co., 1864, 18 illustrations by J. E Millais.
> This is the fifth in the series *Barsetshire Novels.*
> Appeared in Cornhill, Sept., 1862-April 1864, vol. 6-9, (pub. anon. in vol. 6-8, Trollope's name signed in vol. 9.)
> Appeared also in Harper's magazine, Dec. 1862-June 1864, vol. 26-29.
> Pub. also by Harper, N. Y., 1864, 273 p., illus.
> Pub. also in Tauchnitz Collection of British authors, 1864, 3 vols., xii, 917 p.
> Tr. into Dutch: Het Kleine Huis te Allington, uit het Eng., 1866, 3 vols., 3 plates.
> Tr. into French: La Petite Maison d'Allington, tr. de l'anglais par Étienne Marcel, 1866, 2 vols.

Reviews

Howells, W. D., Heroines of *The Warden* and *The Small House,* in Harper's Bazar, April 13, 1901, vol. 34, p. 947-953, 1 illus.

Pattee, Fred L., A history of American literature, 1916, p. 64.

Rhys, Ernest, Introduction to *The Small House at Allington,* 1909, p. vii-viii (Everyman's edition).

Thorold, Algar, Introduction, John Lane New Pocket edition of the *Small House,* 1906.

Washburn, W. T., in North American review, July 1864, vol. 99, p. 292-298.

American Presbyterian and theological review, July 1864, new ser., vol. 2, p. 525-526.

Athenæum, March 1864, no. 1900, p. 437-438.

London Reader, April 2, 1864, vol. 3, p. 418-419.

North American review, July 1861, vol. 93, p. 253-255.

——— ——— Jan. 1865, vol. 100, p. 276-277.

North British review, June 1864, vol. 40, p. 369-401.

Saturday review, May 1864, vol. 17, p. 595-596.

Spectator, April 9, 1864, vol. 37, p. 421-423.

South Africa. In 2 vols. London, Chapman and Hall, 1878. Pub. also in Tauchnitz Collection of British authors, 1878, 2 vols.

Reviews

Trotter, Coutts, in Academy, April 1878, vol. 13, p. 294-296.

Athenæum, Feb. 1878, no. 2625, p. 211-212.

Saturday review, Feb. 1878, vol. 45, p. 241-243.

Spectator, April 1878, vol. 51, p. 445.

Times (Lond.) April 18, 1878, p. 7, col. 1.

——— ——— June 17, 1878, p. 10, col. 2.

South Australia and Western Australia. In 1 vol., 146 p. map. London, Chapman and Hall, 1874.

Separate issue of Part 2 of Trollope's *Australia and New Zealand,* 1873, which see.

The struggles of Brown, Jones and Robinson, by one of the firm. In 1 vol., iv, 254 p. London, Smith, Elder and Co., 1870, 4 illustrations.

Appeared anonymously in Cornhill, Aug. 1861-March 1862, vol. 4-5.

Pub. also by Harper, N. Y., 1862, 136 p.

Reviews

American theological review, 1862, p. 754.

Harper's magazine, June 1862, vol. 25, p. 115.

Thackeray. In 1 vol., vi, 210 p. London, Macmillan and Co., 1879.
One of the English men of letters series, ed. by John Morley.
Tr. into German: William M. Thackeray, frei bearbeitet und mit ammerkungen versehen von L. Katscher, 1880, x, 156 p. (Zierden der englischen literatur in biographischen einzeldarstellungen. bd. 3.)

Reviews

Sala, George A., Things I have seen and people I have known, 1894, vol. 1, p. 2.
Ward, T. H., in Academy, June 1879, vol. 15, p. 533.

Appleton's journal, Aug. 1879, new ser., vol. 7, p. 187-190.
Athenæum, June 1879, no. 2694, p. 749-750.
Contemporary review, 1879, vol. 35, p. 768-769.
Harper's magazine, Aug. 1879, vol. 59, p. 474.
———— ———— Jan. 1881, vol. 62, p. 474.
Nation (N. Y.), Aug. 1879, vol. 29, p. 127-128.
Quarterly review (Lond.), Jan. 1900, vol. 191, p. 148-149, The sentiments of Thackeray.
Scribner's monthly, Aug. 1879, vol. 18, p. 632-633.
Spectator, Sept. 6, 1879, vol. 52, p. 1130-1132.
Westminster review, July 1879, new ser., vol. 56, p. 258.

Thompson Hall. In 1 vol., 127 p. London, Sampson Low and Co., 1885.
An earlier (First) edition pub. under title: Christmas at Thompson Hall, which see for full entry.

The three clerks. In 3 vols. London, Richard Bentley, 1858.
Mr. Chaffanbrass, the lawyer, first appears in this book.
Pub. also by Harper, N. Y., 1860, 497 p.
Pub. also in Asher's Collection of English authors, 187-? 2 vols.

Reviews

Browning, Elizabeth Barrett (in a letter to Mrs. Frances Trollope), in Thomas Adolphus Trollope's What I remember," 2d ed., 1887, vol. 2, p. 188.
Shore, W. Teignmouth, Introduction to the Oxford university press edition of *Three clerks* (World's classics, no. 140), 1907, p. v-xiv.
Thorold, Algar, Introduction, John Lane New Pocket edition of *Three clerks,* 1904, p. v-viii.

American theological review, Aug. 1860, vol. 2, p. 553-554.
Athenæum, Dec. 1857, no. 1574, p. 1621.
Harper's magazine, July 1860, vol. 21, p. 261.
National review, Oct. 1858, vol. 7, p. 416-435.

North British review, June 1864, vol. 40, p. 369-401.
Saturday review, Dec. 1857, vol. 4, p. 517-518.

Travelling sketches. In 1 vol., iv, 112 p. London, Chapman and Hall, 1866.
Reprinted from the Pall Mall gazette.

The two heroines of Plumplington. New York, Harper, 1882.
Appeared also in Good Cheer, Christmas, Dec. 1882 (Christmas supplement to Good Words), p. 1-32, 1 plate, 4 illus.
The Harper edition probably appeared earlier than the publication in Good Cheer.
This story contains an allusion to the celebrated case of the wardenship of Hiram's Hospital, in Trollope's *The Warden.*

La Vendée. In 3 vols. London, Henry Colburn, 1850.
Scene laid in France, covering the years 1792-1800, with retrospect in 1815.
Third Edition, London, Chapman and Hall, 1874, 397 p.
A First Edition offered by E. P. Dutton, New York, in 1923, for $520.00.

Reviews

Athenæum, July 1850, no. 1184, p. 708.
Christian Science monitor, Sept. 19, 1919.

The vicar of Bullhampton. In 1 vol., xvi, 481 p. London, Bradbury, Evans and Co., 1870. 30 illustrations by H. Woods.
Pub. also by Harper, N. Y., 1870, 300 p., 24 illus. by H. Woods.
Pub. also in Tauchnitz Collection of British authors, 1870, 2 vols.
Tr. into Dutch: De predikant van Bullhamton, uit het Eng. door Mw. van Deventer-Busken Huët, 1872, 2 vols.

Reviews

James, Henry, in the Century, 1883, vol. 4, p. 385-395.

Athenæum, April 1870, no. 2218, p. 574.
Harper's magazine, Aug. 1870, vol. 41, p. 459.
Public opinion (London), 1869, vol. 16, Aug. 7, p. 169; Aug. 21, p. 233; Oct. 30, p. 552; Nov. 27, p. 681.
———— ———— 1870, Jan. 8, vol. 17, p. 40.
Saturday review, May 1870, vol. 29, p. 646-647.
Times (Lond.), June 3, 1870, p. 4, col. 3.

Victoria and Tasmania. In 1 vol., 195 p., map. London, Chapman and Hall, 1874.
Separate issue of Part 4 of Trollope's *Australia and New Zealand,* 1873, which see.

The warden. In 1 vol., iv, 336 p. London, Longman, Brown, Green, and Longmans, 1855.

This is the first in the series *Barsetshire Novels.*

Pub. also in Tauchnitz Collection of British authors, 1857 (?), v, 285 p.

Pub also (with *Barchester Towers*) by Harper, N. Y., 1870, 244 p.

Tr. into French: Le gardien, tr. de l'anglais, 1879.

Reviews

Howells, W. D., Heroines of *The Warden,* in Harper's bazar, April 13, 1901, vol. 34, p. 947-953, 1 illus.

Montégut, Émile, Écrivains modernes de l'Angleterre, 1892, vol. 3, p. 1-138, Anthony Trollope, of which article, p. 18-46 are Le roman religieux, *The Warden.*

Thorold, Algar, Introduction, John Lane New Pocket edition of *The Warden,* 1902.

Athenæum, Jan. 1855, no. 1422, p. 107-108.
Christian Science monitor, Sept. 19, 1919.
National review, Oct. 1858, vol. 7, p. 416-435.
North British review, June 1864, vol. 40, p. 369-401.
Old and new, Jan. 1871, vol. 3, p. 109.
Public opinion (Lond.), Feb. 26, 1870, vol. 17, p. 265.
Times (Lond.), May 23, 1859, p. 12, col. 4.

The way we live now. In 2 vols. London, Chapman and Hall, 1875.

Forty illustrations by L. G. F. (Sir Luke Fildes).

Appeared also in part (chapters 1-76), in Old and new, Jan. 1874, vol. 9, to May 1875, vol. 11.

After May 1875, Old and new was merged into Scribner's monthly (later, the Century), and the remaining chapters of the novel (chapters 77-100), were never published in magazine form.

Pub. also by Harper, N. Y., 1875, 408 p., illus.

Pub. also in Tauchnitz Collection of British authors, 1875, 4 vols.

Reviews

Athenæum, Feb. 1874, no. 2418, p. 291.
———— June 1875, no. 2487, p. 851.
Harper's magazine, Oct. 1875, vol. 51, p. 754.
Nation (N. Y.), Sept. 2, 1875, vol. 21, p. 153-154.
Saturday review, July 1875, vol. 40, p. 88-89.
Spectator, June 1875, vol. 48, p. 825-826.
Times (Lond.), Aug. 24, 1875, p. 4, col. 4.
Westminster review, Oct. 1875, new ser., vol. 48, p. 529-530.

The West Indies and the Spanish Main. In 1 vol., iv, 395 p., col. map, London, Chapman and Hall, 1859.

Pub. also by Harper, N. Y., 1860, 385 p.

Pub. also in Tauchnitz Collection of British authors, 1860, v, 320 p.

Two extracts tr. into French by L. Étienne: Les Indes Occidentales, et La Mer des Antilles, par A. Trollope, in Bibliothèque universelle et revue suisse, 1863, n. pér., vol. 16 p. 464-496, 628-663.

Reviews

Athenæum, Nov. 1859, no. 1671, p. 591-593.

Chamber's journal, Dec. 3, 1859, ser 3, vol. 12, p. 363-365.

Harper's magazine, July 1860, vol. 21, p. 260-261.

North American review, Jan. 1860, vol. 90, p. 289.

Quarterly review (London), Oct. 1860, vol. 108, p. 103 ff.

Saturday review, Nov. 1859, vol. 8, p. 643-645.

Same article in Littell's, Jan. 28, 1860, vol. 64, p. 209-212.

———— ———— Dec. 1859, vol. 8, p. 675-676.

Times (Lond.) Jan. 6, 1860, p. 4, col. 2.

———— ———— Jan. 18, 1860, p. 12, col. 1.

II. SHORT STORIES

Alice Dugdale, and other stories. In 1 vol., 287 p., Leipzig, Tauchnitz, 1883.
In Tauchnitz Collection of British authors, no. 2154.

Contents

Lady Dugdale.
See full entry with title *Alice Dugdale,* in *Why Frau Frohman raised her prices, and other stories,* 1882.

Aaron Trow.
See full entry in *Tales of all countries,* 2d Series, 1863.

The O'Conors of Castle Conor.
See full entry in *Tales of all countries,* 1st Series, 1861.

Relics of General Chassé.
See full entry in *Tales of all countries,* 1st Series, 1861.

The Château of Prince Polignac.
See full entry in *Tales of all countries,* 1st Series, 1861.

George Walker at Suez.
See full entry in *Tales of all countries,* 2d Series, 1863.

An editor's tales. In 1 vol., 375 p. London, Strahan and Co., 1870.

Contents

The Turkish bath.
Appeared also in St. Paul's magazine, Oct. 1869, vol. 5, p. 110-128.
Appeared also in Galaxy, Nov. 1869, vol. 8, p. 689-703.
Appeared also in Littell's, Dec. 25, 1869, vol. 103, p. 807-817.

Mary Gresley.
Appeared also in St. Paul's, 1869, vol. 5, p. 237-256.

Josephine de Montmorenci.
Appeared also in St. Paul's, Dec. 1869, vol. 5, p. 366-384.
Appeared also in Galaxy, Dec. 1869, vol. 8, p. 825-839.

The Panjandrum.
Appeared also in St. Paul's, Jan.-Feb. 1870, vol. 5, p. 434-453, 562-577.
Appeared also in Galaxy, Feb.-Mar. 1870, vol. 9, p. 252-266, 333-345.

The Spotted Dog.
Appeared also in St. Paul's, March-April, 1870, vol. 5, p. 669-688; vol. 6, p. 58-77.

Appeared also in Galaxy, April-May, 1870, vol. 9, p. 497-
511, 611-625.
Appeared also in Littell's, April-May, 1870, vol. 105,
p. 272-283, 355-366.

Mrs. Brumby.
Appeared also in St. Paul's, May 1870, vol. 6, p. 181-199.

Reviews

Athenæum, July 1870, no. 2230, p. 112.
Contemporary review, 1870, vol. 15, p. 319.
Graphic (Lond.), Aug. 20, 1870, vol. 2, p. 183.
Public opinion (Lond.), Aug. 13, 1870, vol. 18, p. 199.
Saturday review, Aug. 1870, vol. 30, p. 211-212.
Spectator, Oct. 1870, vol. 43, p. 1203-1205.

Frau Frohmann, and other stories, 1883.
For full entry, see earlier edition under title *Why Frau
Frohmann raised her prices, and other stories,* 1882.

Fred Pickering, and other stories.
Pub. in Asher's collection of English authors, 1868? 331 p.
See full entry, with title *Adventures of Fred Pickering,* in
Lotta Schmidt, and other stories, 1867.

The gentle Euphemia; or, Love shall still be lord of all.
In Fortnightly review, 8 p., May, 1866, vol. 4, p. 692-699.

The Lady of Launay.
For earlier edition, see full entry in Section I. Single works.

Lotta Schmidt, and other stories. In 1 vol., 403 p., London,
Alexander Strahan, 1867.
This is considered to be the 3d of the series *Tales of all
countries.*

Contents

Lotta Schmidt.
Appeared also in Argosy (Lond.), July 1866, vol. 2,
p. 130-146.
Tr. into French: Lotta Schmidt; scènes de la vie vien-
noise, 28 p., in Bibliothèque universelle et revue suisse,
1866, n. pér., vol. 26, p. 412-439.
Adventures of Fred Pickering.
Appeared also, with title *Misfortunes of Fred Pickering,*
in Argosy (Lond.), Sept. 1866, vol. 2, p. 292-306.
The Two Generals.
Appeared also in Good words, 1863, p. 853-861.
Father Giles of Ballymoy.
Appeared also (anonymously) in Argosy, May 1866,
vol. 1, p. 511-523.

Malachi's cove.
Appeared also in Good words, 1864, p. 929-936, plate.
Appeared also in Littell's, Jan. 7, 1865, vol. 84, p. 35-44.
Appeared also in English contemporary authors, 1875.
Appeared also in Selected English stories (19th century),
introduction by Hugh Walker, 1920, p. 271-293, (The
World's classics, vol. 193).
Tr. into French: Le baie de Malachi, 23 p., in Biblio-
thèque universelle et revue suisse, 1867, n. pér., vol. 29,
p. 210-232.

The widow's mite.
Appeared also in Good words, 1863, p. 33-43.

The last Australian who left Venice.
Appeared also in Good words, 1867, p. 50-58.

Miss Ophelia Gledd.
Appeared earlier in A Welcome; original contributions
in poetry and prose, 1863, p. 239-283.

The journey to Panama.
Appeared earlier in Adelaide Anne Proctor's Victoria
Regia, 1861, p. 187-214.

Reviews

Athenæum, Nov. 1867, no. 2091, p. 683-684.
Saturday review, Sept. 1867, vol. 24, p. 381-382.
Spectator, Sept. 1867, vol. 40, p. 1062-1063.

La Mère Bauche, and other stories.
Pub. in Tauchnitz Collection of British authors, 1883,
278 p.

Contents

La Mére Bauche.
See full entry in *Tales of all countries,* 1st Series, 1861.

John Bull on the Guadalquiver.
See full entry in *Tales of all countries,* 1st Series, 1861.

Miss Sarah Jack, of Spanish Town, Jamaica.
See full entry in *Tales of all countries,* 1st Series, 1861.

An unprotected female at the Pyramids.
See full entry in *Tales of all countries,* 1st Series, 1861.

Mrs. General Talboys.
See full entry in *Tales of all countries,* 2d Series, 1863.

The man who kept his money in a box.
See full entry in *Tales of all countries,* 2d Series, 1863.

The mistletoe bough, and other stories.
Pub. in Tauchnitz Collection of British authors, 1883, 286 p.

Contents

The mistletoe bough.
See full entry in *Tales of all countries,* 2d Series, 1863.
A ride across Palestine.
See full entry in *Tales of all countries,* 2d Series, 1863.
The courtship of Susan Bell.
See full entry in *Tales of all countries,* 1st Series, 1861.
The Parson's daughter of Oxney Colne.
See full entry in *Tales of all countries,* 2d Series, 1863.
Returning home.
See full entry in *Tales of all countries,* 2d Series, 1863.
The house of Heine Brothers in Munich.
See full entry in *Tales of all countries,* 2d Series, 1863.

Skizzer og novelletter, paa dansk ved L. Kornelius 1885.

Tales of all countries. First series. In 1 vol., 312 p. London, Chapman and Hall, 1861.
The Contents Table of this volume states that *La Mère Bauche* is "Republished from Harper's New York Magazine," also that four of the other stories are "From Cassell's Family Paper."

Contents

La Mère Bauche.
Pub. also, with other stories, in Tauchnitz Collection of British authors, 1883.
The O'Conors of Castle Conor, County Mayo.
Appeared also in Harper's magazine, May 1860, vol. 20, p. 799-806.
Appeared also in Half hours with great novelists, pub. in Chicago, no date, p. 94-130, signed Charles Lever, but given to Trollope in Contents.
Appeared also in W. S. Walsh's Treasure trove series, 1875, vol. 3, p. 94-130, signed Charles Lever, but given to Trollope in Contents.
Appeared also in *Alice Dugdale, and other stories,* 1883.
John Bull on the Guadalquiver.
Appeared also in Cassell's Family paper.
Pub. also in *La Mère Bauche, and other stories,* in Tauchnitz Collection of British authors, 1883.
Miss Sarah Jack of Spanish Town, Jamaica.
Appeared also in Cassell's Family paper.
Pub. also in *La Mère Bauche, and other stories,* in Tauchnitz Collection of British authors, 1883.
The courtship of Susan Bell.
Appeared also in Harper's magazine, Aug. 1860, vol. 21, p. 366-378.

Pub. also in *The mistletoe bough, and other stories,* in
Tauchnitz Collection of British authors, 1883.
Tr. into Swedish: The courtship of Susan Bell skolupl.
med upplysande anmärkningar av O. P. Behm &
Frida Hjertberg, 1912, 55 p.

Relics of General Chassé, a tale of Antwerp.
Appeared also in Harper's magazine, Feb. 1860, vol. 20,
p. 363-370.
Appeared also in *Alice Dugdale, and other stories,* 1883.

An unprotected female at the Pyramids.
Appeared also in Cassell's Family paper.
Pub. also in *La Mère Blanche, and other stories,* in
Tauchnitz Collection of British authors, 1883.

The Château of Prince Polignac.
Appeared also in Cassell's Family paper.
Appeared also in *Alice Dugdale, and other stories,* 1883.

Reviews

Saturday review, Dec. 1861, vol. 12, p. 587-588.
——— ——— Feb. 1863, vol. 15, p. 276-278.
Same article in Littell's, 28 March 1863, vol. 76, p. 600-602.

Tales of all countries. Second Series. In 1 vol., 371 p. London, Chapman and Hall, 1863.

Contents

Aaron Trow.
Appeared also in Public opinion (Lond.), 1861, Dec. 14,
p. 266-268; Dec. 21, p. 302-304.
Appeared also in *Alice Dugdale, and other stories,* 1883.

Mrs. General Talboys.
Appeared also in Stories by English authors: Italy, 1896,
p. 137-175.
Pub. also in *La Mère Bauche, and other stories,* in
Tauchnitz Collection of British authors, 1883.

The Parson's daughter of Oxney Colne.
Pub. also in *The mistletoe bough, and other stories,* in
Tauchnitz Collection of British authors, 1883.

George Walker at Suez.
Appeared also in Public opinion, Dec. 28, 1861, p. 333-
336.

The mistletoe bough.
Pub. also, with other stories, in Tauchnitz Collection
of British authors, 1883.

Returning home.
Appeared also in Public opinion (Lond.), in its Literary
suppl., no. 9, Nov. 30, 1861, [4] p., and in the main
magazine, Dec. 7, 1861, p. 234-236.

Pub. also in *The mistletoe bough, and other stories,* in
Tauchnitz Collection of British authors, 1883.

A ride across Palestine.

Pub. also in *The mistletoe bough, and other stories,* in
Tauchnitz Collection of British authors, 1883.

The House of Heine Brothers in Munich.

Appeared also in Public opinion (Lond.), Literary suppl.,
nos. 7 and 8, Nov. 16 and 23, 1861, 4 p. each.

Pub. also in *The mistletoe bough, and other stories,* in
Tauchnitz Collection of British authors, 1883.

The man who kept his money in a box.

Appeared also in Public opinion (Lond.), Literary suppl.,
nos. 5 and 6, Nov. 2 and 9, 1861, 5 and 4 p.

Pub. also in *La Mère Bauche, and other stories,* in Tauchnitz Collection of British authors, 1883.

Reviews

London Reader, 28 Feb. 1863, vol. 1, p. 224.
Saturday review, Feb. 1863, vol. 15, p. 276-278.
Spectator, Extra no. March 7, 1863, vol. 36, p. 20-21.

Thompson Hall. See full entry under title *Christmas at
Thompson Hall,* in Section I, Single works.

The two heroines of Plumplington.

In Good Cheer, Christmas, 1882 (Christmas supplement to
Good Words), p. 1-32, 1 plate, 4 illus.

For earlier edition, see full entry in Section I, Single
works.

Why Frau Frohman raised her prices, and other stories. In
1 vol., vi, 416 p. London, Wm. Isbister, 1882.

Pub. also in Tauchnitz Collection of British authors, with
title: *Frau Frohmann, and other stories,* 1883, 296 p.

A "New Edition" pub. in London, Chatto and Windus,
1892, under the title *Frau Frohmann, and other stories,* vi,
416 p.

Contents

Why Frau Frohmann raised her prices.

Appeared also in Good words, 1887, in 4 parts, 4 illus.

The Lady of Launay.

An earlier (First) edition pub. separately, 1878, 125 p.,
in Harper's half-hour series, vol. 74, which see in
Section I, Single works.

Christmas at Thompson Hall.

An earlier (First) edition pub. separately, 1877, 91 p.,
illus., in Harper's half-hour series, vol. 4, which see in
Section I, Single works.

The telegraph girl.
> Appeared also in Good cheer, Christmas 1877, Christmas suppl. to Good words, p. 1-19, 1 plate, 3 illus.

Alice Dugdale.
> Appeared also in Good cheer, Christmas 1878, Christmas suppl. to Good words, p. 1-31, 1 plate, 5 illus.
>
> Appeared also in *Alice Dugdale, and other stories,* 1883.

Reviews

Critic (N. Y.), July 29, 1882, vol. 2, p. 201.
Harper's magazine, July 1882, vol. 65, p. 317.
Nation (N. Y.), June 15, 1882, vol. 34, p. 504-505.

III. CHRONOLOGICAL LIST OF WORKS

1847 The Macdermots of Ballycloran.
1848 The Kellys and the O'Kellys.
1850 La Vendée.
1855 The Warden.
1857 Barchester Towers.
1858 The three clerks.
      Doctor Thorne.
1859 The Bertrams.
      The West Indies and the Spanish Main.
1860 Castle Richmond.
1861 Framley Parsonage.
      Tales of all countries. First series.
1862 Orley Farm.
      North America.
1863 Tales of all countries. Second series.
      Rachel Ray.
1864 The Small House at Allington.
      Can you forgive her?
1865 Miss Mackenzie.
      Hunting sketches.
1866 The Belton Estate.
      Travelling sketches.
      Clergymen of the Church of England.
      The gentle Euphemia.
1867 Nina Balatka.
      The last chronicle of Barset.
      The Claverings.
      Lotta Schmidt, and other stories.
      (Editor of) Saint Paul's magazine, Oct. 1867-March 1874.
1868 Linda Tressel.
      British sports and pastimes, (Preface and p. 70-129).
      Fred Pickering, and other stories.
1869 Phineas Finn.
      He knew he was right.
      Did he steal it?
1870 The Vicar of Bullhampton.
      An editor's tales.
      The struggles of Brown, Jones and Robinson.
      The commentaries of Cæsar.

1871 Sir Harry Hotspur of Humblethwaite.
Ralph the heir.

1872 The Golden Lion of Granpere.

1873 The Eustace diamonds.
Australia and New Zealand.

1874 Phineas Redux.
Lady Anna.
Harry Heathcote of Gangoil.
Australia and New Zealand re-issued in four separate
vols.:
New South Wales and Queensland.
South Australia and Western Australia.
New Zealand.
Victoria and Tasmania.

1875 The way we live now.

1876 The Prime minister.

1877 The American senator.
Christmas at Thompson Hall.

1878 South Africa.
Is he Popenjoy?
How the "Mastiffs" went to Iceland.
The Lady of Launay.

1879 An eye for an eye.
Thackeray.
John Caldigate.
Cousin Henry.

1880 The Duke's children.
The life of Cicero.

1881 Dr. Wortle's school.
Ayala's angel.

1882 Why Frau Frohmann raised her prices, and other stories
Lord Palmerston.
Kept in the dark.
Marion Fay.
The fixed period.
The two heroines of Plumplington.

1883 Mr. Scarborough's family.
The landleaguers.
The Autobiography.
Alice Dugdale, and other stories.
La Mère Bauche, and other stories.
The mistletoe bough, and other stories.
Frau Frohmann, and other stories.

1884 The old man's love.

1892 Frau Frohmann, and other stories. New ed.

1923 The noble jilt (written in 1850).

IV. CONTRIBUTIONS TO MAGAZINES, ETC.

Appleton's journal.
A walk in the woods, Nov. 1879, new ser., vol. 7, p. 452-457. Reprinted from Good words, 1879, p. 595-600.

Athenæum (London).
American literary piracy, letter to William (i.e. James?) Russell Lowell, Cambridge, Mass., Sept. 1862, no. 1819, p. 306-307. Discussion continued Sept.-Oct. 1862.

Letters and discussion, in defence of T. A. Trollope's statement in regard to the Pope's Swiss guards, Dec. 6, 1862, no. 1832, p. 730-731; Dec. 27, 1862, no. 1835, p. 848; Jan. 3, 1863, no. 1836, p. 24; Jan. 10, 1863, no. 1837, p. 60.

British sports and pastimes, ed. by Anthony Trollope.
On hunting, 1868, p. 70-129.

Cornhill magazine.
W. M. Thackeray, Feb. 1864, vol. 9, p. 134-137.
Same article in Thackeray the humorist and man of letters ... by Theodore Taylor, (pseud. of John Camden Hotten), to which is added In memoriam, by Charles Dickens, and a sketch by Anthony Trollope, pub. by D. Appleton, New York, 1864, p. 232-242.

Eclectic magazine.
Charles Dickens, Sept. 1870, new ser., vol. 12, p. 297-301. Reprinted from St. Paul's magazine, July 1870, vol. 6, p. 370-375.

Fortnightly review.
On anonymous literature, 1865, vol. 1, p. 491-498.
The Irish church, 1865, vol. 2, p. 82-90.
Public schools, 1865, vol. 2, p. 476-487.
The civil service, 1865, vol. 2, p. 613-626.
The fourth commandment, Jan. 1866, vol. 3, p. 529-538.
Mr. Freeman on the morality of hunting, Dec. 1, 1869, vol. 12, p. 616-625.
>   And see an article on the above by Helen Taylor, entitled: A few words on Mr. Trollope's defence of fox-hunting, Jan. 1870, vol. 13, p. 63-68.

Cicero as a politician, April 1877, vol. 27, p. 495-515.
Cicero as a man of letters, Sept. 1877, vol. 28, p. 401-422.
Kafir Land, Feb. 1878, vol. 29, p. 191-206.

Iceland, Aug. 1878, vol. 30, p. 175-190.
The same pub. also under title: *How the "Mastiffs" went to Iceland,* privately printed in 1878.
George Henry Lewes, Jan. 1879, vol. 31, p. 15-24.
Same article in Littell's, Feb. 1, 1879, vol. 140, p. 307-313.

Good words.
The young women in the London Telegraph office, 1877, p. 377-384.
In the hunting field, 1879, p. 98-105, 1 illus.
A walk in the wood, 1879, p. 595-600.
Same article in Appleton's journal, Nov. 1879, new ser., vol. 7, p. 452-457.
And see an article entitled: A famous novelist's modes of work, (largely a quotation of Trollope's *A walk in the wood*), in London Society, 1883, vol. 44, p. 347, port.

Littell's Living age.
George Henry Lewes, Feb. 1, 1879, vol. 140, p. 307-313.
Reprinted from Fortnightly, Jan. 1879, vol. 31, p. 15-24.
Novel reading; the works of Charles Dickens and W. Makepeace Thackeray, Feb. 8, 1879, vol. 140, p. 349-361.
Reprinted from Nineteenth century, Jan. 1879, vol. 5, p. 24-43.

Nineteenth century.
Novel reading; the works of Charles Dickens and W. Makepeace Thackeray, Jan. 1879, vol. 5, p. 24-43.
Same article in Littell's, Feb. 8, 1879, vol. 140, p. 349-361.

North American review.
The genius of Nathaniel Hawthorne, Sept. 1879, vol. 129, p. 203-222.
Henry Wadsworth Longfellow, April 1881, vol. 132, p. 383-406.

St. Paul's magazine.
Charles Dickens, July 1870, vol. 6, p. 370-375.
Same article in Eclectic, Sept. 1870, new ser., vol. 12, p. 297-301.

Swedish translations.
Disponenten af . . . Förf. till *"Doctor Thorne," "The Bertrams,"* etc., öfversättning fran engelskan, in Nytt kabinets bibliothek af in- och utlandsk roman-litteratur, 1859, h. 26-31, 250 p.

Times (London).
A letter from Trollope, written March 2, 1864, to Sir Rowland Hill, on his great postal success, Dec. 1, 1883, p. 7, col. 6.

The Luxemburg route to Basle. Nov. 27, 1874, p. 6, col. 6;
Dec. 10, 1874, p. 6, col. 6.
Complaints against the railway service on that line.

Transactions of the National association for the promotion of social science.

Manchester meeting, 1866 (published 1867), vol. 10, p. 119-
125; Discussion, p. 243-244, On the best means of extend-
ing and securing an international law of copyright.

V. BOOK REVIEWS WRITTEN BY TROLLOPE

Fortnightly review.

Henry Taylor's Poems, 1865, vol. 1, p. 129-146.

John Ruskin's Sesame and lilies, 1865, vol. 1, p. 633-635.
And see an article by Sir Edward T. Cook, entitled:
The life of John Ruskin, 1911, vol. 2, p. 94.

James Hannay's Characters and criticisms, 1865, vol. 2, p. 255-256.

Capt. W. A. Baker's The day and the hour, 1865, vol. 2, p. 379-380.

Charles Buxton's The ideas of the day on policy, Jan. 15, 1866, vol. 3, p. 650-652.

Alberto Mario's The red shirt, Feb. 1, 1866, vol. 3, p. 775-777.

R. H. Hutton's Studies in Parliament, April 1, 1866, vol. 4, p. 510-512.

Sir M. Peto's Resources and prosperity of America, May 15, 1866, vol. 5, p. 126-128.

Goldwin Smith's The Civil war in America, June 1, 1866, vol. 5, p. 251-254.

John Ruskin's The crown of wild olives, June 15, 1866, vol. 5, p. 381-384.

Harriet Parr's The life and death of Jeanne d'Arc, Nov. 1, 1866, vol. 6, p. 632-636.

Mrs. Sewell's The rose of Cheriton, Feb. 1, 1867, vol. 7, p. 252-255.

George Rooper's Flood, field and forest, June 1, 1869, vol. 11, p. 748-750.

VI. NOTICES OF LECTURES

Public opinion (London), Nov. 22, 1873, Mr. Anthony Trollope. *On novels.*
Short report of a speech delivered Nov. 13, 1873, at the annual presentation of prizes to students at the Liverpool Institute.

Times (London), Nov. 14, 1873, p. 10, col. 3, *The teaching of novels.*
Report of a speech by Trollope, Nov. 13, 1873, at the annual distribution of prizes to the students of Liverpool Institute.

―――― ―――― March 4, 1876, p. 11, col. 3, Mr. Trollope on the *Art of reading.*
Report of an address delivered March 2, 1876, at the Second annual distribution of prizes to students of the Quebec Institute.

―――― ―――― Nov. 29, 1876, p. 6, col. 5, Mr. Anthony Trollope *On reading.*
Report of an address delivered Nov. 28, 1876, at the annual distribution of prizes to the students of the City and Spitalfields School of art.

VII. BIBLIOGRAPHIES

[**Anthony Trollope.**] Catalogue of his books, 8vo., n. p.
1874. Presentation copy with inscription, in the South Ken-
sington museum, Science and art department of the Com-
mittee of council on education, Forster collection.

Sargent, G. H. In Boston evening transcript, Dec. 11, 1912.

Lavington, Margaret. In Escott, T. H. S. Anthony Trollope, 1913, p. 309-336.

Sadleir, Michael. Excursions in Victorian bibliography,
1922, p. 37-73.

VIII. BIOGRAPHY AND CRITICISM

Much general criticism on Trollope is to be found also in the Reviews listed under "The Autobiography."

Aitken, Robert. In Chamber's Cyclopædia of English literature, New ed., 1921-22, vol. 3, p. 486-490, port.

Aldred, Thomas. List of English and American sequel stories, 1922, p. 66.

Austin, Alfred. Autobiography, 1911, vol. 1, p. 166, 180; vol. 2, p. 23-24.

———— ———— The garden that I love.
This work of Austin's was inspired by a visit to Trollope's Sussex home, Hartley Grange.
Authority: T. H. S. Escott's Anthony Trollope, 1913, p. 300.

Baker, Ernest A. Guide to the best fiction in English, 1913, p. 91-93.

———— ———— History in fiction, 1906, vol. 1, p. 126.

Barker, Frederick. In Manchester quarterly, 1899, vol. 18, p. 210-299.

Barot, Odysse. Histoire de la littérature contemporaine en Angleterre, 1874, p. 134, 270, 414, 479.

Barran, John N. In Nation and the Athenæum (Lond.), May, 1924, vol. 35, p. 173.

Bede, Cuthbert. Some recollections of Mr. Anthony Trollope. In Graphic (Lond.), Dec. 23, 1882, vol. 26, p. 707.

Benjamin, Lewis S. Victorian novelists, 1906, p. 168-187, port.
Reprinted from the Author (London).

Bennett, Arnold. Books and persons, 1917, p. 134-135, 139, 148-149).

Bettany, F. G. In praise of Anthony Trollope's novels, in Fortnightly, June, 1905, v. 83, p. 1000-1011.
Same article in Littell's, July 15, 1905, vol. 246, p. 166-176.

Bidwell, Alice T. The places of England. 1924, p. 135.

Bidwell, W. H. In Eclectic, June, 1880, vol. 94, p. 760-761, port.

Biron, Sir Henry Chartres. In National review. 1920. v. 75, p. 76-88.
Same article in Littell's, April 1920, vol. 305, p. 165-175.
Reprinted in Biron, Sir H. C., Pious opinions, 1923, p. 261-282.

Bleibtreu, Karl. Geschichte der englischen literatur. 1923, p. 306.

Boucher, Léon. Histoire de la littérature anglaise. 1890, p. 496.

Boyd, Andrew K. H. Twenty-five years of St. Andrews. 2d ed. London, 1892, vol. 1, p. 100-101.
Very disparaging comment on Trollope's personality and manner.

Bradford, Gamaliel. American portraits, 1922, p. 176.

—— —— Bare souls, 1924, p. 247.

—— —— A naturalist of souls, 1926, p. 135-154.
Reprinted from Atlantic monthly, March 1902, vol. 89, p. 426-432.

—— —— Portraits of American women, 1919, p. 125.

Braithwaite, William Stanley. Anthony Trollope, 100 years old and still alive; the foundation of his steady fame reviewed on the centenary of his birth, in Boston Evening transcript, April 24, 1915, p. 4 and 7, port.

Brawley, Benjamin Griffith. A new survey of English literature, 1925, p. 326.

Brickdale, Eleanor F. Golden book of famous women. 1919, p. 191-194, Mrs. Proudie.

Bryce, James. The death of Anthony Trollope, in Nation (N. Y.), Jan. 1883, vol. 36, p. 10-11.

—— —— Merits and defects of Trollope, in Bryce's Studies in contemporary biography, 1903, p. 116-130.

Buchan, John. A history of English literature. 1923, p. 506-507.

Burton, Richard, Charles Dickens, 1919, p. 245, 251, 261.

—— —— Masters of the English novel, 1909, p. 252-258, also frequent mention, see index.

Byrde, Margaretta. In Sewanee review, 1922, vol. 30, p. 324-325.
A criticism of Professor Phelps's opinion that Alexander Marshall is a worthy successor of Trollope.

Campbell, D. R. Peculiarities of genius, in Author (Boston), 1889, vol. 1, p. 62.

Canby, Henry Seidel. Better writing, 1926, p. 17 and 82.

——— ——— The feminine touch in literature, in Vassar quarterly, June 1926, vol. 11, p. 174.

Cazamian, L. Époques moderne et contemporaine, pt. 2 of E. H. Legouis's Histoire de la littérature anglaise, 1924, p. 1142-1143, 1193.

Cazamian, Madaleine L. Le roman et les idées en Angleterre, Paris, 1923, p. 5-9, 57-59, and see index.
Thesis, Strasbourg, Faculté des lettres.

Chancellor, E. Beresford. Literary diversions, 1925, p. 113-120. Trollope and the Barsetshire novels.

Chapman, Robert W. The portrait of a scholar, 1920, p. 112, 122.

Chesterton, Gilbert R. The Victorian age in literature, 1913, p. 132-133.

Chevalley, Abel. Le roman anglais de notre temps, 1921, p. 36-37.

——— ——— The modern English novel, tr. by B. R. Redman, 1925, p. 37-38.

Clemens, Samuel L. Mark Twain's autobiography, 1924, vol. 2, p. 231.

Compton-Rickett, Arthur. A history of English literature, 1919, p. 516-517.

Cook, Sir Edward Tyas. The life of John Ruskin, 1911, vol. 2, p. 94.
On Trollope's review of Sesame and lilies, pub. in Fortnightly review, 1865, vol. 1, p. 633-635.

Cooke, Jane G. In Warner library of the world's best literature, University ed., 1917, vol. 25, p. 15031-15056, port.

Cooper, Thompson. Men of the time, 1875, p. 959.

——— ——— Men of mark, 1878, vol. 3, p. 2, photograph no. 2.

Courtney, W. P. The secrets of our national literature (anonymous writings), 1908, p. 98-99.

Cousin, John W. A short biographical dictionary of English literature. (Everyman's library), 1921, p. 385.

Cracroft, Bernard. The morality of field sports, in Spectator, Jan. 8, 1870, vol. 43, p. 46-47.

Croal, Thomas A. A book about travelling, past and present. London, 1877, illustrated.
Contains an illustrated article on Irish mails and Trollope.
Authority, a 1926 Book-sales catalogue.

Cross, Wilbur L. The development of the English novel, 1920, p. 215-224, and see index.

Crowell's handbook for readers and writers, 1925.
Contains notes on Trollope's works and principal characters, alphabetically arranged.

Cushing, Harvey. The life of Sir William Osler, 1925, vol. 1, p. 664-672; vol. 2, p. 602.

Dickens, Charles. Letter to T. A. Trollope, Dec. 1868, on Anthony Trollope's becoming a candidate for Beverley. In Trollope, T. A., What I remember. 2d ed. 1887, vol. 2, p. 128-129.

Didier, Eugene L. In Author (Boston), 1889, vol. 1, p. 18.

Dobson, Austin. At Prior Park, and other papers. (World's classics) 1925, p. 105.
For further notes on Dobson, see under Gosse, Sir Edmund.

Downey, Edmund. Charles Lever, his life in his letters. 1906, vol. 1, p. 294 foot-note; vol. 2, p. 227, 232.

Drew, Elizabeth A. The modern novel, 1926, p. 20, 135.

Drinkwater, John. The outline of literature, 1924, vol. 3, p. 826-827.

Durrett, Florence. The Irish question as portrayed in the fiction of 1800-50.
Columbia University M. A. thesis, 1924.

Edwards, Amelia B. The art of the novelist, in Contemporary review, Aug. 1894, vol. 66, p. 225-242.
Same article in Littell's, Sept. 22, 1894, vol. 202, p. 771-883.

Egan, Maurice F. Return to the quiet novel, in Bookman (N. Y), Sept. 1921, vol. 54, p. 17-23.
An article on Alexander Marshall.

—— —— Confessions of a book-lover, 1922, p. 153-154, 169-172, and see index.

Elton, Oliver. Survey of English literature from 1830-80, 1920, vol. 2, p. 276-282, and see index.

Emerson, Edward Waldo. The early years of the Saturday club, 1918, p. 257-258.

Engel, Edward. Geschichte der englischen literatur, 1915, p. 453-454.

Escott, T. H. S. England, 1880, p. 532-533.

—— —— In Fortnightly review, Dec. 1906, new ser., vol. 80, p. 1096-1104.

—— —— In Quarterly review, Jan. 1909, vol. 210, p. 210-230. Same article in Littell's, May 22, 1909, vol. 261, p. 459-472.

—— —— Masters of English journalism, 1911, p. 238, 244.

—— —— Social transformations of the Victorian age, 1897, p. 11-12.

—— —— Anthony Trollope, his work, associates, and literary originals, 1913, xvi, 351 p., port, 2 plates.
Issued also with title, Anthony Trollope, his public services, private friends, and literary originals, 1913, xvi, 351 p., port., 2 plates.
Both editions pub. by John Lane, London, New York.

—— —— National and international links, 1922, p. 278.

Field, Kate. Last days of Walter Savage Landor, in Atlantic monthly, June, 1866, vol. 17, p. 698.

Firkins, Oscar W. William Dean Howells, 1924. See index.

Fitzpatrick, W. J. The life of Charles Lever. 1879, vol. 2, p. 269-270, 320, 408.

Fletcher, Robert H. A history of English literature, 1919, p. 442.

Frazer, Barbara. The social work of the clergy . . . in early 19th century fiction.
Columbia University M. A. thesis, 1924.

Freeman, Edward A. In Macmillan's, Jan. 1883, vol. 47, p. 236-240.
Same article in Littell's, Jan. 1883, vol. 156, p. 177-181.
Same article in Eclectic, March 1883, vol. 100, p. 406-410.

Friswell, J. Hain. Modern men of letters honestly criticised, 1870, p. 133-144.

Fry, Henry Walter. Trollope's novels, in Times (N. Y.), Sunday, June 12, 1921, Section VII, p. 12, col. 2.

Fuller, Henry B. Review of Sir Arthur Quiller-Couch's Charles Dickens and other Victorians, in Times (N. Y.), Book review, Sunday, Aug. 30, 1925, p. 4, port.

Furniss, Harry. Some Victorian men, 1924, p. 37-40, port.

Garnett, Richard. In Dictionary of national biography, 1899, vol. 57, p. 238-242.

——— ——— English literature, an illustrated record (vol. 4 by Edmund Gosse), 1904, vol. 4, p. 319-321, port.

Gissing, George. The private papers of Henry Ryecroft, 1914, p. 212-216.

Goldring, Douglas. London news letter, in New York tribune, Magazine section, Sunday, Nov. 18, 1923, p. 29, col. 4. On Hugh Walpole's coming critical study of Anthony Trollope.

Gorman, Herbert S. A successor to Trollope (Archibald Marshall), in Times (N. Y.), Sunday book review, June 26, 1921, p. 18, col. 1-5.

Gosse, Edmund. A short history of modern English literature, 1900, p. 371.

——— ——— In Richard Garnett's English literature, an illustrated record, 1904, vol. 4, p. 319-321, port.

——— ——— Austin Dobson, in Quarterly review, Jan. 1922, vol. 237:
On page 56: "Anthony Trollope published, in St. Paul's magazine, a poem of Dobson's, which marked a sudden advance in the poet's career."
On page 57: "Dobson published his first book, 'Vignettes in rhyme,' in 1873 (English edition), dedicated to Anthony Trollope."

——— ——— Silhouettes, 1925, p. 189.

Graham, Bessie. The bookman's manual, 2d ed., 1924, p. 385-386.

Greenlaw, Edward A. A syllabus of English literature, 1914, p. 302.

Gwynn, Stephen. In Macmillan's, Jan. 1900, vol. 81, p. 217-226.

———— ———— Trollope in Ireland, in Contemporary review, Jan. 1926, vol. 129, p. 75-79.
Same article in Littell's, March 6, 1926, vol. 328, p. 539-544.

Hardman, Sir William. A mid-Victorian Pepys, 1923, p. 143-144.

Harries, Frederick J. Famous writers and Wales, 1925, p. 141-142.

Harrison, E. B. The Victorian woman, in Nineteenth century, Dec. 1905, p. 953.

Harrison, Frederic. Anthony Trollope's place in literature, in Forum, May 1895, v. 19, p. 324-337.
Same article in his Studies in early Victorian literature, 1895, p. 200-225.
Same article in 2d ed., 1897, p. 183-204.

———— ———— Among my books, 1912, p. 110.

———— ———— Introduction to the *Barsetshire Novels,* London, Bell, 1913-14, 8 vols. (Bohn's popular library).

———— ————De senectute, 1923, p. 3, 27.

Harter, Eugene W. The future of Trollope, in Bookman (N. Y.), April 1905, vol. 21, p. 137-141.

Harwood, H. C. In London Mercury, July, 1920, vol. 2, p. 292-303.

Hawk, Affable. In New statesman, April 22, 1922, vol. 19, p. 67.

Hawthorne, Julian. The maker of many books, in Manhattan, 1883, vol. 2, p. 573-578.
Same article in his Confessions and criticisms, 1887, p. 140-162.

Hawthorne, Nathaniel.
A much-quoted extract on the subject of Trollope, written by Hawthorne, in a letter to an American gentleman, is given in an article by Trollope, called *The genius of Nathaniel Hawthorne,* in the North American review, 1879, vol. 129, p. 205.
The same is given in a Biographical sketch of Hawthorne, by George Parsons Lathrop, to be found in Hawthorne's Complete works, vol. 12, Tales, sketches, and other papers, Boston, 1886, p. 539-540.

——— ——— Complete works, vol. 9, Passages from the American note-books, Boston, 1886, p. 8.

Heywood, J. C. How they strike me, these authors, 1877, p. 78-96. A novelist who means business, Anthony Trollope.

Higginson, Thomas Wentworth. Cheerful yesterdays. 1899, p. 287.

Holliday, Carl. English fiction, 1912, p. 355-357.

Hovey, Carl. The life story of J. Pierpont Morgan, 1912, p. 341.

Howells, William D. My literary passions, 1895, p. 219, 247.

Hudson, W. H. A short history of English literature in the nineteenth century, 1918, p. 231, 236, 254-255.

James, Henry. In Century, July 1883, vol. 4, new ser., p. 385-395, port.

——— ——— Partial portraits, 1888, p. 95-133.

Jefferson, Joseph. Autobiography, 1890, p. 314.
"And to be glared at through the fierce but honest spectacles of Anthony Trollope was a treat indeed."

Jordan, Mary A. Criticism of T. H. S. Escott's Anthony Trollope, Yale review, April 1914, new ser., vol. 3, p. 607-611.

Keller, Helen Rex. Reader's digest of books, 1922, p. 71, 650, and see index.

Kellner, Leon. Englischen literatur im zeitalter Königin Viktoria, 1909, p. 232-237, and see index.

——— ——— A second edition of the above: Die englische literatur der neuesten zeit, 1921, p. 132-135, and see index.

Knox, Ronald A. A ramble in Barsetshire, in London Mercury, Feb. 1922, vol. 5, p. 378-385, map.
Contains a map of Barsetshire, constructed by Mr. Knox.

Laing, Frederick A. A history of English literature, 1873, p. 201.

Lathrop, George Parsons. Biographical sketch of Hawthorne, in Hawthorne's Complete works, vol. 12, Tales, sketches and other papers, 1886, p. 539-540.

Legouis, E. H. Histoire de la littérature anglaise, 1924; Pt. 2, Époques moderne et contemporaine, par L. Cazamian, p. 1142-1143, 1193.

Lever, Charles.
For Lever's opinion of Trollope, see entries under Downey, Edmund: Fitzpatrick, W. J.: Mumby, F. A.

Ley, J. W. T. The Dickens circle. 2d ed. 1916, p. 75-76.

Littledale, R. T. Obituary of Anthony Trollope, in Academy, Dec. 1882, vol. 22, p. 433.

Long, William J. Outlines of English and American literature, 1917, p. 311, 313.

Lord, Walter F. The novels of Anthony Trollope, in Nineteenth century, May 1901, vol. 49, p. 805-816.
This article was reprinted in Lord's The mirror of the century, 1906, p. 231-251.

——— ——— The mirror of the century, 1906, p. 203-208, 231-251, 256-258, also frequent mention.

MacDonagh, Michael. In the throes of composition, in Cornhill, Nov. 1904, new ser., vol. 17, p. 607-627.
Same article in Littell's, Dec. 24, 1904, vol. 243, p. 776-791.

McGill, Anna B. Some famous literary clans; III, The Trollopes, in Book buyer, Oct. 1900, vol. 21, p. 195-203, port, and a caricature (p. 201) erroneously ascribed to Fred Walker. It is by Frederick Waddy.

Macleod, Donald. Anthony Trollope, obituary, in Good words, 1884, p. 248-252, port.

Macy, John. The story of the world's literature, 1925, p. 362-363.

Magnus, Laurie. English literature in the 19th century, 1909, pp. 256-257.

Mathew, E. J. A history of English literature, 1901, p. 507-511, and see index.

Matz, B. W. "Phiz"; the centenary of Hablot Knight Browne, in Bookman (London), June, 1915, v. 48, p. 69-74.

Mirsky, D. S. Contemporary Russian literature, 1926, p. 34-35.

Montégut, Émile. Écrivains modernes de l'Angleterre, 1892, vol. 2, p. 1-138.

Moody, William Vaughn. A history of English literature, Rev. ed., 1918, p. 411-412.

Morley, Henry. First sketch of English literature, 1896, p. 943-944, 1070.

Morris, Mowbray. Anthony Trollope, a poem, in Graphic (Lond.), Dec. 30, 1882, vol. 26, p. 719.

Motley, John Lothrop. Correspondence, 1889, vol. 2, p. 265.

Muirhead, Findlay. England, 2d ed. (Blue guides), 1924, p. 64.
  "At Harting Anthony Trollope lived in 1880-82."

Muirhead, James F. W. D. Howell's, the American Trollope, in Landmark (Lond.), Dec. 1920, vol. 2, p. 812-816, Jan. 1921, vol. 3, p. 53-56.
  Same article in Littell's, Jan. 1921, vol. 308, p. 304-309.

Mumby, Frank Arthur. Letters of literary men. 1906, p. 507.
  Charles Lever's opinion of Trollope.

Nevins, Allan. American social history as recorded by British travellers, 1923, p. 159, 294.

―――― ―――― Trollope's novels, in New York evening sun, The book column, June 30, 1924.

Newbolt, Sir Henry. An English anthology of prose and poetry, 1922, vol. 2, p. 74.

Newton, A. Edward. The amenities of book-collecting, 1920, p. 75, 111-112, 249-266, port., A great Victorian.

―――― ―――― The ghosts of Gough Square, in Atlantic monthly, June 1925, vol. 135, p. 818-825 (Trollope p. 824).
―――― ―――― The greatest book in the world, and other papers, 1925. p. 70, 270, 322, 326, 339-340.

Nichols, Spencer Van Bokkelen. The significance of Anthony Trollope, 1925, 59 p., port., caricature, map.
  Edition of 490 numbered copies.

Nicoll, Henry J. Landmarks of English literature, 1883, p. 401-402.

Nield, Jonathan. A guide to the best historical novels and tales, 1911, p. 125-126.

Oliphant, Mrs. Margaret O. W. In Good words, 1883, p. 142-144.
  Same article in Littells, April 1883, vol. 156, p. 507-510.
  Same article in Eclectic, April 1883, vol. 100, p. 531-534.

―――― ―――― Success in fiction, in Forum, May, 1889, vol. 7, p. 314-322.
  Same article in Author (Boston), 1889, vol. 1, p. 70-72.

―――― ―――― The Victorian age of English literature, 1892, vol. 2, p. 471-477.

Paterson, Isabel. Anthony Dare, by Archibald Marshall in New York tribune, Sunday magazine, Nov. 4, 1923, p. 22. A few words of comparison between Marshall and Trollope.

Patterson, Mabel. Through the year with famous authors, 1925, p. 98-99.

Paul, Herbert. The apotheosis of the novel under Queen Victoria, in Nineteenth century, May, 1897, v. 41, p. 769-792. Same article in Littell's, June 19, 1897, vol. 213, p. 779-796.

Payn, James. Some literary recollections, 1884, p. 166-168, 180.

Payne, G. H. E. Belles lettres in ballot boxes; a forgotten statesman, Plantagenet Palliser, in Forum, 1925, vol. 73, Jan., p. 107-110, Feb. p. 249-252.

Pearce, Nina McClure. The Barchester novels of Anthony Trollope. 54 p.
Columbia University M. A. thesis, 1924.

Peck, Harry Thurston. In Bookman (N. Y.), April, 1901, vol. 13, p. 114-125, port.
Same article reprinted in his Studies in several literatures, 1909, p. 165-197.

Perry, Bliss. A study of prose fiction, Rev. ed., 1920. See index.

Phelps, William Lyon. The advance of the English novel, 1916, p. 59, 115-116.

—— —— Archibald Marshall, realist, in North American review, June 1918, vol. 207, p. 891-901 (on Trollope, p. 895-896).

Pollock, Walter Harris. In Harper's magazine, May 1883, vol. 66, p. 907-912, port.

Priestley, John Boynton. George Meredith, 1926, p. 161, 163.

Quiller-Couch, Sir Arthur. Charles Dickens and other Victorians; Anthony Trollope; the *Barsetshire Novels,* 1925, p. 219-334, and see index.
This article appeared first in the Nation and the Athenæum (Lond.), 1924, vol. 35, May 3, p. 142-144; May 10, p. 173-175.

Raleigh, Sir Walter. Letters, 1926, vol. 1, p. 7, 272.

Randell, W. L. In Fortnightly, Sept. 1920, vol. 114, p. 459-467.

Ritchie, Hester. Letters of Anne Thackeray Ritchie, 1924, p. 125, 233-234.

Russell, Frances T. Satire in the Victorian novel, 1920, (Frequent mention, see index.)

Russell, Percy. A guide to British and American novels, 1894, p. 154-156.

Sadleir, Michael. Excursions in Victorian bibliography, 1922, p. 1-73, comprising an introductory essay (p. 1-36), and a list of Trollope's First Editions (p. 37-73), with bibliographical details.
Same article as the above Introductory Essay, but with title, A guide to Anthony Trollope, in Nineteenth century, April 1922, vol. 91, p. 648-658.

—— —— Introduction to the *Autobiography* (Oxford university press, World's classics, no. 239), 1923, pref. p. v-xvi.

—— —— Why only Dickens? In Nation and the Athenæum (Lond.), Feb. 9, 1924, vol. 34, p. 667-668.

—— —— Anthony Trollope and his publishers, in Library (Lond.), Dec. 1924, series 4, vol. 5, p. 215-242.
Read before the Bibliographical society, Nov. 17, 1924.

—— —— The Victorian woman as Trollope knew her, in The Bermondsey book (Lond.), March 1925, vol. 2, p. 14-22.

Saintsbury, George. Corrected impressions, 1895, p. 172-177. Three mid-century novelists: Charlotte Brontë, George Eliot, and Anthony Trollope.

—— —— Later nineteenth century, 1907, p. 82, 120-122, 359-362.

—— —— The English novel, 1913, p. 250-253, and see index.

—— —— Trollope revisited, in Saintsbury's Collected essays and papers, 1923, vol. 2, p. 312-343 (preceded, p. 284-287, by a reprint of his remarks on Trollope in his Three mid-century novelists, with footnote, p. 287, of apologetic confession).
This article appeared first in English association, Essays and studies, 1920, vol. 6, p. 41-66.

—— —— History of 19th century literature (1700-1900), 1925, p. 339-341.

—— —— Short history of English literature, 1925, p. 750-751.

Sala, George Augustus. Echoes of the year 1883, 1884, p. 17-18.

―――― ―――― Things I have seen and people I have known, 1894, vol. 1, p. 30-31.

Scudder, Horace Elisha. James Russell Lowell, 1901, vol. 2, p. 82-84.

Seccombe, Thomas. In Bookman (Lond.), June, 1915, vol. 48, p. 65-69, illus., ports.
    Same article in Littell's, July 27, 1915, vol. 286, p. 167-173.

Sedgwick, Alice. In National review, March, 1910, vol. 55, p. 94-103.
    Same article in Littell's, April 9, 1910, vol. 265, p. 74-80.

Seward, Frederick W. Reminiscences of a war-time states-man and diplomat, 1916, p. 190.

Shaylor, Joseph. Sixty years a bookman, 1923, See index.

Sherman, Stuart P. Men of letters of the British Isles, 1924, p. 123.
    In an article on Hugh Walpole.

Sichel, Walter. The sands of time, 1924 ,p. 217-219, 223.
    Contains (p. 218), a "Sketch by Millais, probably to illus-trate one of Trollope's novels."

Simonds, William E. A student's history of English litera-ture, 1902, p. 428-429.

Smalley, G. W. Recollections, in McClure's, Jan. 1903, vol. 20, p. 298-299, port. on p. 300.

Speare, Morris E. The political novel, 1924, p. 185-220, 334.

Spencer, Walter T. Forty years in my bookshop, 1923, p. 15-16, 58, 78, 199-200.

Stack, J. Herbert. In Fortnightly, Feb. 1869, vol. 11, p. 188-198.

Stephen, Leslie. In National review, Sept. 1901, vol. 38, p. 68-84.
    Same article in Littell's, Nov. 9, 1901, vol. 231, p. 366-378.
    Same article in Eclectic, 1902, vol. 138, p. 112-124.
    Same article reprinted in Stephen's Studies of a biographer, 1902, vol. 4, p. 168-205.

Stevens, Clarence D. Introduction to *Barchester Towers*, 1923, xviii pref. p. (Modern student's library, published by Scribner.)

Stoddard, R. H. In Critic (N. Y.), July 16, 1881, vol. 1, p. 193, port. (on p. 183).

—— —— In Harper's weekly, Dec. 16, 1882, vol. 26, p. 805, port.

Street, G. S. In Cornhill, March 1901, v. 83, p. 349-355. Same article in Littell's, April 13, 1901, vol. 229, p. 128-133. Same article reprinted in Street's A book of essays, 1902, p. 198-212.

Swinburne, Algernon Charles. Miscellanies: Essay on Charles Reade, 1886, p. 296-300.

—— —— Studies in prose and poetry, 1894, p. 94, 111.

Symonds, J. A. The Renaissance in Italy and England, in Quarterly review, Jan. 1878, p. 27-29.

Taintor, S. A. Training for secretarial practice, 1923, p. 293. "List of novels containing secretaries among their characters." Trollope, A. *Three clerks; Small House at Allington; Last chronicle of Barset; Duke's children; John Caldigate; Mr. Scarborough's family; Marion Fay.*

Thorold, Algar. Introductions to several of the John Lane New Pocket Edition of Trollope's novels, 1902-06.

Tooker, Lewis Frank. The joys and tribulations of an editor, 1924, p. 11.

Towle, G. M. In Appleton's journal, May 14, 1870, vol. 3, p. 551-553, port.

—— —— A novelist of the day, in Appleton's journal, Sept. 1879, new ser., vol. 7, p. 275-278.

Traill, H. D. New fiction, 1887. Frequent mention of Trollope.

Trent, William P. In Citizen, Nov. 1896, vol. 2, p. 297-298.

Trollope, Frances E. Frances Trollope, her life and literary work, 1895, 2 vols. Frequent mention of Anthony Trollope.

Trollope, Thomas Adolphus. What I remember, 2d ed., 1887, 2 vols. Frequent mention of Anthony Trollope.

Tuckerman, Bayard. A history of English prose fiction, 1882, p. 294-295.

—— —— In Princeton review, July 1883, p. 17-28.

Twain, Mark. See Clemens, Samuel L.

Urban, Sylvanus. Trollope upon novel-writing, in Gentleman's magazine, Jan. 1884, vol. 256, p. 100-101.

Waddy, Frederick. Cartoon portraits and biographical sketches of men of the day, 1874, p. 68-70, caricature.
Same article in Once a week, June 1, 1872, vol. 26, p. 498-501, caricature.

Walker, Hugh. The literature of the Victorian era, 1913, p. 764-765, 772-776, and see index.

——— ——— Outlines of Victorian literature, 1913, p. 140-141, 156.

——— ——— The age of Tennyson, 1921, p. 271-272.

Walpole, Hugh. The English novel, 1925, p. 13, 17-18.

Watkins, Grace Minette. Anthony Trollope's tastes and sympathies as revealed in his English and Irish novels. Columbia University M. A. thesis, 1921.

Webb, W. T.. English of to-day, 1925, p. 19.

Wendell, Barrett. A literary history of America, 1920, p. 176.

Weygandt, Cornelius. A century of the English novel, 1925, p. 97-98, 161-165, 331-332, and see index.

Wharton, Edith. The writing of fiction, 1925, p. 63, 65, 74, 81, 130.

Whiteford, R. N. Motives in English fiction, 1918, p. 325-327, 331-332.

Whyte, Frederic. The life of W. T. Stead, 1925, vol. 1, p. 69.

Willcocks, M. P. Between the old world and the new, 1925, p. 117-127.

Witmer, Eleanor M. "Slaves of the book"; makers and users of books in the Victorian novel. (Frequent mention of Trollope.) Columbia University M. A. thesis, 1925.

Wotton, Mabel E.. Word portraits of famous writers, 1887, p. 313-316.

Wülker, Richard. Geschichte der englischen litteratur, 1896, p. 595.

Yates, Edmund. His recollections and experiences, 1884, 2 vols:
Vol. 1, p. 85, 96, 11, 113-114, 237.
Vol. 2, p. 222-224, 228-233.

—— ——Personal traits of Anthony Trollope, in London world, Feb. 23, 1892.
Written in connection with Andrew K. H. Boyd's sweeping denunciation of Trollope's tone and manner, in his Twenty-five years of St. Andrews, which see.

Young, W. T. In Cambridge history of English literature, 1917, vol. 13, p. 469-472, 620-621, and see indexes in vols. 12-14.

Academy, Jan. 2, 1897, vol. 51, p. 19. From a reader's notebook.

All the year round, Feb. 1884, vol. 33, p. 255-259. Recreations of men of letters.

American book prices current, Index for 1916-22, 1925, p. 1148-1149.

American publishers' circular and literary gazette, May 15, 1863, vol. 1, p. 98-100, Literary piracy.

Appleton's journal, May 14, 1870, vol. 3, p. 551-553, port.

—— —— Sept. 1879, new ser., vol. 7, p. 275-278, A novelist of the day, signed "Time."

Athenæum. Obituary, Dec. 9, 1882, no. 2876, p. 772-773.

—————— Review of T. A. Trollope's What I remember, Nov. 12, 1887, no. 3133, p. 635-636.

—————— Review of T. H. S. Escott's Anthony Trollope, Oct. 4, 1913, no. 4484, p. 337-338.

Atlantic monthly, Sept. 1884, vol. 54, p. 426-428. Anthony Trollope compared with Daudet.

—— —— Aug. 1919, vol. 124, p. 286-287, Barsetshire and the war.

—— —— July 1920, vol. 126, p. 134-136, Trollope and tea.

Blackwood's magazine, Sept. 1867, vol. 102, p. 275-278.
Same article in Littell's, Oct. 5, 1867, vol. 95, p. 16-18.

—— —— March 1879, vol. 125, p. 322-344 (Trollope, p. 338-339).
Same article in Littell's, April 12, 1879, vol. 141, p. 90-106 (Trollope, p. 102).

—— —— Feb. 1883, vol. 133, p. 316, 320.

—— —— April 1891, vol. 149, p. 497-510, Politics in fiction. Same article in Littell's, May 16, 1891, vol. 189, p. 387-397.

—— —— Aug. 1891, vol. 150, p. 233, Names in novels. Same article in Littell's, Sept. 28, 1891, vol. 190, p. 817-818.

Bookman (N. Y.), June 1900, vol. 11, p. 312-313, port.

—— —— June 1903, vol. 17, p. 329-330, illus. (editorial).

—— —— April 1906, vol. 23, p. 125-126, New Trollope series, (by Dodd, Mead and Co.)

—— —— March 1909, vol. 29, p. 1-2, illus., Anthony Trollope's earnings.

—— —— Dec. 1913, vol. 38, p. 348-349, Clara Kellogg's reminiscences: Trollope's methods.

—— —— April 1915, vol. 41, p. 121-125, The Trollope centenary.

Cambridge history of English literature. See indexes in vols. 12-14, 1917-1921, and see entry under Young, W. T. in this Section.

Christian Science monitor, Jan. 23, 1926, p. 11, col. 3-4, Barsetshire mapped; (criticism of) Spencer Van Bokkelen Nichols's The significance of Anthony Trollope.

Contemporary review, 1866, vol. 2, p. 240-262, Mr. Anthony Trollope and the English clergy.

Continent, Aug. 1882, vol., 2, p. 126, 189.

Critic (N. Y.), Jan. 12, 1884, vol. 4 (new ser., vol. 1), p. 22, col. 2.

—— —— Jan. 19, 1884, vol. 4 (new ser., vol. 1), p. 25-27, Last reminiscences of Anthony Trollope. Same article in Littell's, Jan. 26, 1884, vol. 160, p. 248-251. Same article in Temple Bar, Jan. 1884, vol. 70, p. 129-134.

—— —— March 29, 1884, vol. 4 (new ser., vol. 1), p. 155, col. 2.

—— —— June 28, 1884, vol. 4 (new ser., vol. 1), p. 306-307.

Dial, March 1903, vol. 34, p. 141-143. The re-coming of Anthony Trollope.

Dublin review, Oct. 1872, vol. 71 (new ser., no. 38), p. 393-430.

———— ———— April 1883, vol. 92 (3d ser., vol. 9), p. 314-334.

Edinburgh review, Oct. 1877, vol. 146, p. 455-488.

Evening post (N. Y.)) Oct. 28, 1913, p. 8, col. 5-6, Review of
T. H. S. Escott's Anthony Trollope.

———— ———— April 24, 1915, p. 8, col. 4-5, Trollope's centenary.

———— ———— Jan. 21, 1916, p. 8, col. 5-6.

———— ———— June 26, 1917, p. 8, col. 5, Death of Mrs. Anthony
Trollope.

———— ———— Aug. 30, 1919, p. 8, col. 4-5, Novelists and their
personages.

———— ———— Aug. 6, 1923, p. 6, col. 5-6.

Every Saturday, May 28, 1870, new ser., vol. 1, p. 347-349.
The parson of Mr. Trollope's novels.

Graphic (London), Dec. 16, 1882, vol. 26, p. 661, port.

Harper's magazine, Sept. 1897, vol. 59, p. 630.
Review of Thackeray's Henry Esmond, containing Trollope's opinion of the book.

Illustrated London news, Dec. 16, 1882, vol. 81, p. 618-619,
622, 646, port. on p. 620.

Lincoln library of essential information, 1924, p. 221, 1989.

Literary digest, Aug. 14, 1915, vol. 51, p. 310, To Anthony
Trollope (poem).

Literary world (Boston), Dec. 1882, vol. 13, p. 456.
———— ———— March 1900, vol. 31, p. 72.

Littell's Living age, Oct. 5, 1867, vol. 95, p. 16-18.
Reprinted from Blackwood's, Sept. 1867, vol. 102, p. 275-278.

———— ———— Feb. 6, 1869, vol. 100, p. 379-381, The empire of
novels.
Reprinted from Spectator, Jan. 9, 1869, vol. 42, p. 43-44.

———— ———— April 12, 1879, vol. 141, p. 90-106 (Trollope, p.
102).
Reprinted from Blackwood's, March 1879, vol. 125, p. 322-
344 (Trollope, p. 338-339.)

———— ———— Jan. 20, 1883, vol. 156, p. 186-189, From Miss
Austen to Mr. Trollope.
Reprinted from Spectator, Dec. 16, 1882, vol. 55, p. 1609-
1611.

———— ———— Dec. 1, 1883, vol. 159, p. 573-575, Anthony Trollope as a critic.
Reprinted from Spectator, Oct. 27, 1883, vol. 56, p. 1373-1374.

———— ———— Jan. 26, 1884, vol. 160, p. 248-251, Last reminiscences of Anthony Trollope.
Reprinted from Critic (N. Y.), Jan. 19, 1884, vol. 4 (new ser., vol. 1), p. 25-27.

———— ———— Feb. 21, 1885, vol. 164, p. 478-503, English character and manners as portrayed by Anthony Trollope.
Reprinted from Westminster review, Jan. 1885, vol. 123 (new ser., vol. 67), p. 53-100.

———— ———— April 26, 1890, vol. 185, p. 235-242, On the meaning of novels.
Reprinted from Macmillan's, March 1890, vol. 61, p. 372-380.

———— ———— May 16, 1891, vol. 189, p. 387-397, Politics in fiction.
Reprinted from Blackwood's, April 1891, vol. 149, p. 497-510.

———— ———— Sept. 28, 1891, vol. 190, p. 817-818, Names in novels.
Reprinted from Blackwood's, Aug. 1891, vol. 150, p. 233.

———— ———— Dec. 4, 1897, vol. 215, p. 627-637, Treatment of dissent in English fiction.
Reprinted from London Quarterly review (pub. by C. H. Kelly), Oct. 1897, vol. 89 (new ser., vol. 29), p. 54-72.

———— ———— Oct. 30, 1909, vol. 263, p. 290-294.
Reprinted from Times (London), Literary supplement, Sept. 9, 1909, p. 321, col. 2.

———— ———— Nov. 6, 1909, vol. 263, p. 369-371, Mid-Victorian church and chapel.
Reprinted from Nation (N. Y.), Sept. 15, 1909, vol. 5, p. 910-911.

———— ———— Dec. 9, 1911, vol. 271, p. 626-629, Mid-Victorian chronicle.
Reprinted from Nation (N. Y.), Oct. 14, 1911, vol. 10, p. 86-87.

———— ———— March 29, 1924, vol. 320, p. 620-621.
Reprinted from Saturday review, Feb. 16, 1924, vol. 137, p. 151-152.

London Quarterly review, (C. H. Kelly, pub.), Oct. 1897, vol. 89, (new ser., vol. 29), p. 54-72, Treatment of dissent in English fiction.
Same article in Littell's, Dec. 4, 1897, vol. 215, p. 627-637.

London society, 1883, vol. 44, p. 347-353, port., A famous novelist's modes of work.

London Speaker, Supplement, May 2, 1896, p. 488. Review of Frances Eleanor Trollope's Frances Trollope, her life and literary work.

Macmillan's magazine, March 1890, vol. 61, p. 372-380, On the meaning of novels.
Same article in Littell's, April 26, 1890, vol. 185, p. 235-242.

Nation (N. Y.), Sept. 25, 1909, vol. 5, p. 910-911, Mid-Victorian church and chapel.
Same article in Littell's, Nov. 6, 1909, vol. 263, p. 369-371.

——— ——— Oct. 14, 1911, vol. 10, p. 86-87, Mid-Victorian chronicle.
Same article in Littell's, Dec. 9, 1911, vol. 271, p. 626-629.

National review, Oct. 1858, vol. 7, p. 416-435.

North British review, May, 1864, vol. 40, p. 369-401.

Notes and queries, Feb. 22, 1873, 4th ser., vol. 11, p. 156, Proper order of the *Barchester Novels.*
(on the same subject), April 29, 1893, 8th ser., vol. 3, p. 329.
(on the same subject), May 6, 1893, 8th ser., vol. 3, p. 352.

——— ——— Oct. 13, 1906, 10th ser., vol. 1, p. 288, Note on John Trollope, living Nov. 1700.

——— ——— Oct. 3, 1914, 11th ser., vol. 10, p. 280, Note of a commemorative tablet affixed to 39 Montague Square, by the London County Council.

Philadelphia Ledger, Oct. 24, 1902, Anthony Trollope's methods.
"Reprinted from Pall Mall magazine."

Publishers' circular (London), Jan. 17, 1925, vol. 122, p. 51-52, 1 illus., "Vanity Fair" and Anthony Trollope.

Quarterly review (London, John Murray, pub.), Jan. 1878, vol. 145, p. 27-29.

——— ——— Oct. 1894, vol. 179, p. 546, Novels of adventure and manners.

Saturday review, Nov. 1873, v. 36, p. 656-657. Mr. Trollope on novels.

——— ——— Dec. 9, 1882, vol. 54, p. 755-756, Obituary.

—— —— Feb. 16, 1924, vol. 137, p. 151-152.
Same articles in Littell's, March 29, 1924, vol. 320, p. 620-621.

Spectator, Nov. 2, 1867, vol. 40, p. 1219, Mr. Trollope retires from the Post Office.

—————— Jan. 9, 1869, vol. 42, p. 43-44. The empire of novels.
Same article in Littell's, Feb. 6, 1869, vol. 100, p. 379-381.

—————— Dec. 4, 1869, vol. 42, p. 1421-1422, The morality of coursing.

—————— Dec. 2, 1876, vol. 49, p. 1499, Mr. Trollope's ideas on the power of reading.

—————— Dec. 9, 1882, vol. 55, p. 1565.

—————— Dec. 9, 1882, vol. 55, p. 1573-1574, Death of Anthony Trollope.

—————— Dec. 16, 1882, vol. 55, p. 1609-1611, From Miss Austen to Mr. Trollope.
Same article in Littell's, Jan. 20, 1883, vol. 156, p. 186-189.

—————— Oct. 20, 1883, vol. 56, p. 1343-1344, Boyhood of Anthony Trollope.

—————— Oct. 27, 1883, vol. 56, p. 1373-1374, Anthony Trollope as a critic.
Same article in Littell's, Dec. 1, 1883, vol. 159, p. 573-575.

Sun (Evening sun, N. Y.), May 14, 1913, p. 13, col. 4-5, Reading Trollope.

Sun (Morning sun, N. Y.), March 28, 1915, Section III, p. 10, col. 8. The Trollope centenary; a novelist who disclosed the secrets of his workshop.

Temple Bar, Jan. 1884, vol. 70, p. 129-134, Last reminiscences of Anthony Trollope.
Reprinted from Critic (N. Y.) Jan. 19, 1884, vol. 4 (new ser., vol. 1), p. 25-27.

Times (London), Nov. 2, 1867, p. 9, col. 6, Dinner to Anthony Trollope.

—— —— May 4, 1875, p. 11, col. 2, Trollope in Ceylon.

—— —— June 18, 1877, p. 11, col. 16, Anthony Trollope, the novelist en route for the Cape.

—— —— Illness of Trollope (almost daily reports from Nov. 6-Dec. 6, 1882).

—— —— Literary supplement, Sept. 9, 1909, p. 321-322. Same article in Littell's, Oct. 30, 1909, vol. 263, p. 290-294.

—— —— Literary supplement, Sept. 18, 1913, p. 386, col. 3, Review of T. H. S. Escott's Anthony Trollope.

—— —— April 6, 1914, p. 13, col. 4, Memorial tablet to be affixed to 39 Montagu-Place.

—— —— May 30, 1917, p. 36, Death of Mrs. Anthony Trollope.

—— —— Literary supplement, March 20, 1919, p. 153, col. 1, Ullathorne Court.

—— —— May 8, 1922, Literary supplement, p. 16, col. 5, Review of Michael Sadleir's Excursions in Victorian bibliography.

—————— Literary supplement, Oct. 15, 1925, p. 671, The Trollopian faith; review of Spencer Van Bokkelen Nichols's The significance of Anthony Trollope.

Times (N. Y.), Saturday review of books and art, March 16, 1901, p. 168, col. 3-4.

—— —— Nov. 30, 1913, Sunday, Section VI, p. 673, col. 3.

—— —— April 4, 1915, Sunday, Section VI, p. 124, col. 2.

—— —— April 25, 1915, Sunday. Section III, p. 2, col. 4.

—— —— Sunday, June 5, 1921, p. 2, cols. 4-5 (editorial), The unflattering glass.

—— —— Book review, Sunday, Jan. 18, 1925, Section III, p. 13, col. 1, port. Review of Harry Furniss's Some Victorian men.

—— —— Book review, Sunday, Aug. 30, 1925, Section III, p. 4, port. Review by Henry B. Fuller, of Sir Arthur Quiller-Couch's Charles Dickens and other Victorians.

Tribune (N. Y.), Dec. 7, 1822, p. 2, col. 4, Trollope (obituary, with list of works).

—— —— Dec. 9, 1882, p. 4, col. 3 Trollope's work (editorial).

—— —— Dec. 24, 1882, p. 4, col. 6, How Trollope worked. Reprinted from the London Standard.

—— —— Oct. 28, 1883, p. 6, col. 2, Trollope and civil service reform.

—— —— Sunday Book Section, Sept. 21, 1924, p. 16, col. 1, Review of Anthony Wharton's Be good, sweet maid.

—— —— Sunday Book Section, Oct. 18, 1925, p. 19, For Trollope collectors; review of S. Van Bokkelen Nichols's The significance of Anthony Trollope.

Vanity Fair album, April 15, 1873, vol. 5 (text opposite caricature no. 50).

Westminster review, Jan. 1883, new ser., vol. 63, p. 287.

—— —— Jan. 1885, vol. 123 (new ser., vol. 67), p. 53-100, English character and manners as protrayed by Anthony Trollope.
    Same article in Littell's, Feb. 21, 1885, vol. 164, p. 478-503.

IX. POEMS

Gosse, Sir Edmund, Austin Dobson, in Quarterly review, Jan. 1922, vol. 237:
On page 56: "Anthony Trollope published, in St. Paul's magazine, a poem of Dobson's, which marked a sudden advance in the poet's career."
On page 57: "Dobson published his first book, 'Vignettes in rhyme,' in 1873 (English edition), dedicated to Anthony Trollope."

Morris, Mowbray, Anthony Trollope, a poem, in Graphic (Lond.), Dec. 30, 1882, vol. 26, p. 719.

Literary digest, To Anthony Trollope (Poem), Aug. 14, 1915, vol. 51, p. 310.

X. PORTRAITS

Those not otherwise described are simply head and shoulders.

Group I.—From photographs by Elliott and Fry.

Trollope's Autobiography, New York, Harper, 1883, Frontispiece.
Seated, showing down to waist-line.

Benjamin, Lewis S., Victorian novelists, 1906, p. 168.
Seated, showing down to below knees, with hands in pockets.

Bookman (N. Y.), June 1900, vol. 11, p. 312.

—— —— April 1901, vol. 13, p. 116, with autograph, article by Harry Thurston Peck.

—— —— April 1906, vol. 23, p. 124, Article on the New Trollope series of Dodd, Mead and Company.
Chamber's cyclopædia of English literature, New ed., 1921-22, vol. 3, p. 487.

Good words, 1884, p. 249.
Similar to the portrait in Garnett's English literature.

Graphic, Dec. 16, 1882, vol. 26, p. 661.
Seated, showing down to waist-line, with hands in pockets.

Harper's monthly, May 1883, vol. 66, p. 908, article by Walter Harris Pollock.
Seated, showing down to waist-line, with hands in pockets.

London society, 1883, vol. 44, p. 347, article on "A famous novelist's modes of work."
Seated, showing down to waist-line, with hands in pockets.

McClure's magazine, Jan. 1903, vol. 20, p. 300, article by G. W. Smalley, Recollections.
Seated, showing down to below knees, hands not in pockets.

Group II.—From photographs by Elliott and Fry.

Engraved by Leopold Lowenstam.

Trollope's Autobiography, London, William Blackwood, 1883, vol. 1, Frontispiece with autograph.

——— ——— New York, Dodd, Mead, 1905. Frontispiece, with autograph.

——— ——— London, Oxford univ. press, 1923, Frontispiece, with autograph.

Book buyer, Oct. 1900, vol. 21, p. 197, with autograph, article by Anna B. McGill, Some famous literary clans: The Trollopes.

Garnett's English literature, 1904, vol. 4, p. 319, with autograph.

Newton, A. Edward, The amenities of book-collecting, 1920, p. 250, with autograph: article on "A great Victorian."

Nichols, Spencer Van Bokkelen, The significance of Anthony Trollope, 1925, p. 11, with autograph.

Times (N. Y.), Book review, Sunday, Aug. 30, 1925, p. 4, Review of Sir Arthur Quiller-Couch's Charles Dickens and other Victorians, by Henry B. Fuller.
The Lowenstam engraving, but without the autograph.

Group III.—From a drawing by Samuel Lawrence, made in 1864, in possession of Mrs. Anthony Trollope.

Braithwaite, William Stanley, Anthony Trollope 100 years old and still alive, in Boston Evening transcript, April 24, 1915, p. 4 and 7, port. on p. 4.

Escott, T. H. S., Anthony Trollope, 1913, Frontispiece.

Lord, W. F., Mirror of the century, 1906, Frontispiece.

Group IV.—Miscellaneous sources.

Appleton's journal, May 14, 1870, vol. 3, p. 552, article by G. M. Towle.
Similar to port. in Harper's weekly, which see.

Bookman (London), June 1915, vol. 18, article by Thomas Seccombe. On page 65, a port. of Trollope (from phot. by Window and Grove); on page 67, a port. of Frances Trollope (from miniature by Hervieu).

Century magazine, July 1883, vol. 26 (new ser., vol. 4), p. 384, article by Henry James.
Full length, standing, coat wide open with very much white vest, "Drawn by R. Birch, after a photograph by Sarony."
Similar port. in Critic (N. Y.), which see.
Similar port. in Trollope's *Prime minister,* Boston, Estes and Lauriat, no date, Frontispiece, which see.

Christian Science monitor, Aug. 29, 1923, p. 14, Review of the *Noble Jilt,* signed E. F. H.
Signature on portrait: S. W. W.

Critic (N. Y.), July 16, 1881, vol. 1, p. 183, accompanies an article "The Trollopes," by R. H. Stoddard on page 193.
Portrait is signed "Blum del. 1881," is similar to the portrait in Century, which see, but showing only to the knees.

Eclectic magazine, June 1880, vol. 94, p. 641.
"Engraved for the Eclectic by J. J. Cade, New York."

Furniss, Harry, Some Victorian men, 1924, p. 38.
Port. signed: Hy F. (i.e. Harry Furniss).
This is somewhat of a caricature.

Galaxy, Oct. 1871, vol. 12, p. 451.

Harper's weekly, Dec. 16, 1882, vol. 26, p. 805, article by R. H. Stoddard.
Similar to the portrait in Appleton's journal, which see.

Illustrated London news, Dec. 16, 1882 ,vol. 81, p. 620, accompanies editorial articles on p. 618-619, 622, 646.
"From a portrait by the London Stereoscopic company."

The Lamp (later the Book buyer), Jan. 1905, p. 644.
Full length, standing, with cane, wearing hat; trousers so wide and long at the foot as to sweep the ground.
"From the collection of Robert Coster."

New York Public Library, no date.
Signed: Butterworth, Heath and Co.
In the collection of Trollope portraits in possession of the New York Public Library.

Times (N. Y.), Sunday Book review, Jan. 18, 1925, Section III, p. 13, col. 1. Review of Harry Furniss's Some Victorian men, 1924.
Port. signed: Hy F (i.e. Harry Furniss).

Trollope's "How the 'Mastiffs' went to Iceland." London,
Virtue and co., 1873. Privately printed.
   Illustrations by Mrs. Hugh Blackburn, col. map., 14
pencil drawings lithographed, 2 photographs.
   In six of these drawings Trollope figures prominently.
He is represented also in one of the photographs, but very
indistinctly.

Trollope's "Prime minister," Boston, Estes & Lauriat, no
date of pub., Frontispiece.
   Full face, open coat, white vest, showing down to waist-
line. Similar to portrait in the Century, which see.
   "From a photograph from Life."

Trollope's "Three clerks," World's classics edition, Oxford
University press, 1907, Frontispiece.

Warner's library of the world's best literature, 1917, vol. 25,
p. 15031, article by Jane G. Cooke.

Wilson, Thomas Walter
   Photographic copy of "A memorable whist party at the
Athenæum: Anthony Trollope, W. E. Forster, Abraham
Hayward, Sir George Jessel." Signed: T. Walter Wilson.
(In possession of M. L. Irwin.) See frontispiece of this
volume.

XI. PHOTOGRAPHS

Cooper, Thomas, Men of mark, 1878, vol. 3, photograph
no. 2.
  Photographed from life by Lock and Whitfield.

Small photograph, 4 x 2½ inches, full length, standing;
photographer, Herbert Watkins, London.
  In possession of M. L. Irwin.

XII. CARICATURES

Book buyer, Oct. 1900, vol. 21, p. 201, article by Anna B.
McGill, Some famous literary clans: III, The Trollopes.
Erroneously ascribed to Fred Walker. It is by Frederick Waddy (see reference under Waddy).

Furniss, Harry. Some Victorian men, 1924, p. 38.
Port. signed: Hy F. (i.e. Harry Furniss).
This is somewhat of a caricature.

Nichols, Spencer Van Bokkelen, The significance of Anthony
Trollope, 1925, p. 34.
Reproduction of the caricature in Vanity Fair, which see.

Once a week, June 1, 1872, vol. 26, p. 499.
Caricature by Frederick Waddy (see reference under
Waddy).

Publishers' circular, Jan. 17, 1925, vol. 122, p. 51.
Reproduction of caricature in Vanity Fair, which see.

Punch Feb 5, 1881, p. 58, by Linley Sambourne.
Shows Trollope embracing a bust of Cicero, which is
crowned with a modern silk tile.
Inscription: Antonius Trollopius, author of The Last
chronicles of Cicero.
"O rare for Antony!"—Shakespeare.
Punch's fancy portraits, no. 17.

Sem. Original caricature portrait of Trollope, by Sem (size
10 in. by 7 in.), entitled at top "Sem's Pantheon-Authors,"
and at bottom "Anthony Trollope," full figure, facing front,
holding transversely a large quill pen.

Vanity Fair album, 1873, vol. 5, no. 231.
In colors.

Waddy, Frederick, Cartoon portraits, 1874, p. 68.
Shows Trollope seated on a pile of books, manipulating
the strings of a jointed doll, which is dressed as a bishop.

XIII. ILLUSTRATIONS

Bookman (London), June 1915, vol. 48, article by Thomas Seccombe.

On page 66, an illustration by Millais, of the farmhouse at Harrow, used in *Orley Farm.*

On page 67, portrait of Mrs. Frances Trollope, from a miniature by Hervieu.

On pages 67 and 68, two illustrations by Hablot K. Browne, for *Can you forgive her?*

They were probably for vol. 2, and not used, as vol. 2 was illustrated by Miss Taylor. The illustrations are entitled:

(1) "The Captain for the first time in his life tasted perfect bliss."

(2) "The tramps."

Bookman (N. Y.), June 1903, vol. 17, p. 330.

"Wealdstone farmhouse where Anthony Trollope spent the most miserable period of his life."

"This landmark is about to be destroyed."

——— ——— March 1909, vol. 29, p. 2, article on "Anthony Trollope's earnings."

House at Waltham.

Cincinnati Public library.

Woodcut of Mrs. Frances Trollope's Bazaar in Cincinnati, built 1828-1829, demolished in 1881.

In possession of the Cincinnati Public library.

Escott, T. H. S., Anthony Trollope, 1913, p. 2 and 288.

Hastings Grange.

Garnett's English literature, 1904, vol. 4, p. 320.

House in Montagu Square.

Harper's bazar, April 13, 1901, vol. 34, article by W. D. Howells, Heroines of *The Warden,* and *The Small House.* Illus. by George T. Tobin.

Page 946, "Eleanor Harding in *The Warden.*"

Page 951, "So she (Lily Dale) sat, with her eyes fixed on the open window."

——— ——— June 1901, vol. 35, p. 102, article by W. D. Howells, Anthony Trollope's Mrs. Proudie.

"'This will not do at all,' she said." (Drawn by Henry Hutt.)

Herald (N. Y.), Sat., Aug. 8, 1914, p. 8, col. 4-6, "Lest we forget." Intimate studies of the great novels of the good old times. Anthony Trollope and *Barchester Towers.* Illustration of Mrs. Proudie.

Sichel, Walter, The sands of time, 1924, p. 218. "Sketch by Millais, probably to illustrate one of Trollope's novels."

XIV. MAPS OF BARSETSHIRE

Trollope's Autobiography, 1883, (last lines of the Eighth chapter):
"Framley Parsonage . . . was the fourth novel of which I had placed the scene in Barsetshire, and as I wrote it, I made a map of the dear county. . . ."
Spencer Van B. Nichols, in his The significance of Anthony Trollope, 1925, says:
"This map which Trollope writes of in his *Autobiography* was left among his papers . . . and is now in possession of Mr. Michael Sadleir."

Knox, Ronald A., A ramble in Barsetshire, in London Mercury, Feb. 1922, vol. 5, p. 378-385.
Contains on p. 379, a map constructed by Mr. Knox.

Nichols, Spencer Van Bokkelen, The significance of Anthony Trollope, 1925.
Frontispiece, a folded map, constructed by George F. Muendel, with illustrations in color.

XV. AUTOGRAPHS

Morley, Henry, Of English literature in the reign of Victoria, 1882, p. xxxiv.
Facsimile autograph written in 1874.

The following Autographs are signed on portraits.

Trollope's Autobiography, London, Blackwood, 1883, vol. 1, Frontispiece.

—— —— New York, Dodd, Mead, 1905, Frontispiece.

—— —— London, Oxford univ. press, 1923, Frontispiece.

Book buyer, Oct. 1900, vol. 21, p. 197, article by Anna B. McGill, Some famous literary clans; III, The *Trollopes*

Bookman (N. Y.), June 1900, vol. 11, p. 116, article by Harry Thurston Peck.

Garnett's English literature, 1904, vol. 4, p. 319.

Newton, A. Edward, The amenities of book-collecting, 1920, p. 250.

Nichols, Spencer Van Bokkelen. The significance of Anthony Trollope, 1925, p. 11.

XVI. LETTERS

Original letter, Feb. 3, 1864. Waltham House, Waltham Cross.
To "My dear Smith," 3 p.
Catalogue of John Smith and Sons (Glasgow), Ltd., March 1924.

Original letter. 1867. Waltham Cross.
To Mrs. Macquoid, 2 p.
Sold, London, Dec. 21, 1921   £1
(Autograph prices current, vol. 6.)

Letter, Oct. 3, 1869, to Alfred Austin on his "Vindication of Lord Byron," in Austin's Autobiography. 1911, vol. 2, p. 6.

Original letter. April 22, 1871. Waltham Cross.
To Mr. Fields, the publisher, about Trollope's proposed trip to Australia, 2½ p.
Estate of George D. Smith, New York, Catalogue of sale, Feb. 10, 1923.

Letter, May 5, 1871, to Alfred Austin, as Trollope was leaving for Australia, in Austin's Autobiography, 1911, vol. 2, p. 19.

Original letter. Aug. 20, 1871. 3 p., "I think I left my umbrella in your house."
Catalogue of John Smith and Son (Glasgow), Ltd., 1923.

Original letter. April 12, 1878. 3 p., Advising a friend as to certain political endeavors.
Sold, London, May 29, 1918.
(Autograph prices current, vol. 3)   10s.

Facsimile letter. April 12, 1878. 39 Montagu Square
To Mr. Trübner.
In Garnett's English literature, 1904, vol. 4, p. 321.
Criticism of a book on ostriches.

Original letter. July 24, 1878. 39 Montagu Square, 4 p.
Sold, March 29, 1916, N. Y., $5.50
(American book-prices current.)

Original letter. Nov. 16, 1878. 39 Montagu Square, 4 p.
Sold, April 28, 1914, N. Y., $8.00
(American book-prices current.)

A sheaf of Victorian letters written to Thomas Hardy, among which are some of Trollope's.
Sold, London, April 28, 1916.   £15 10s.
(Autograph prices current, vol. 1.)

XVII. BOOK-PLATES

Facsimile of Trollope's book-plate, engraved about 1860, in Castle, Egerton. English book-plates, 1892, p. 128.

Description of Trollope's book-plate, quoted from a Sales catalogue, in Slater, J. H. Book-plates and their value: English and American plates, 1898, p. 225.

Description of Trollope's book-plate, in Journal of the Ex Libris Society, July 1894, vol. 4, p. 105. "Plain armorial. Owner's name in full. No signature. No date. No motto. Badly engraved; generally on coloured paper."

XVIII. ORIGINAL MANUSCRIPTS

American Senator.
Autograph ms., about 800 p.
Sold, N. Y., March 29, 1916. $585.00
   (American book-prices current.)

——— ——— Sold, N. Y., Feb. 17, 1919. $660.00

Belton Estate.
Original holograph ms., 620 p.
Sold, London, April 4, 1917. £9
   (Autograph prices current, vol. 2.)

——— ——— Sold, N. Y., Feb. 9, 1920. $425.00
   (American book-prices current.)

California sketches.
Original ms., in pencil, with a letter to Trübner. Typed
   transcript, N. Y., 1875, 8 p.
Sold, N. Y., Nov. 27, 1922. $120.00
   (American book-prices current.)

The Duke's children.
Holograph ms., 105 p.
Sold London, April 22, 1918. £32
This ms. is now in the private library of Mr. A. Edward
   Newton of Philadelphia.

He knew he was right.
Original ms. is in the private library of Mr. J. Pierpont
   Morgan, New York City.

Lady Anna.
Original holograph ms., over 700 p.
Presented by Mr. Henry M. Trollope, to be sold for the
benefit of the British Red Cross Society, and the Order of
the Hospital of St. John of Jerusalem in England.
Sold, London, April 26, 1916. £28
   (Book-prices current.)

North America.
Original ms., 1220 p., bound in 2 vols.
Sold, London, March 1906. £71
   (Book-prices current.)

——— ——— Sold, London, July 27, 1911. £120
   (Book-prices current.)

——— ——— Sold, London, March 27, 1923. £70
   (Book-auction records.)

Orley Farm.
Ms. of over 1000 p., With autograph letter by Trollope to Mr. Chapman, and a letter from Mr. Chapman stating that the ms. is in Trollope's writing throughout.
Sold, N. Y., Nov. 19, 1919. $710.00
(American book-prices current.)

Rachel Ray.
Original holograph ms., about 300 sheets of paper, written on both sides.
With receipt for purchase by John Lane, signed by Henry M. Trollope, the son of the novelist.
Catalogue of Mrs. John Lane's library, sold, London, April 16, 1926. £210

Ralph the heir.
Original autograph ms., 792 p. Written on both sides. Bound in 2 vols.
Sold, Philadelphia, June 26, 1919. $650.00
(American book-prices current.)
—— —— Sold, Dec. 20, 1920. $190.00
(Book-prices current.)
—— —— Sold, April 22, 1924. $450.00
(Book-prices current.)
This ms. is now in the private library of Mr. A. Edward Newton of Philadelphia.

South Africa.
Original holograph ms. signed on title, dated 1878, 753 p.
Sold, London, April 28, 1916. £4
(Autograph prices current, vol. 1.)
—— —— Sold, N. Y., Feb. 9, 1920. $375.00
(American book-prices current.)

Vicar of Bullhampton.
Original holograph ms., about 380 sheets of paper, written on both sides.
With receipt of purchase by John Lane, signed by Henry M. Trollope.
Catalogue of Mrs. John Lane's library, sold, London, April 16, 1926. £300

Way we live now.
Original ms., 1212 p. With eighteen of the original pen-and-ink drawings by Sir Luke Fildes. Bound in 2 vols.
Sold, N. Y., May 24, 1916. $590.00
(American book-prices current.)

XIX. SALES AND PRICES OF FIRST EDITIONS

Authorities:

American Book-Prices Current, New York.
Book-Auction Records, London.
Book-Prices Current, London.

I.—Collected Works.

April 1895. Works, 1st ed. 122 vols.

Sold, New York, $307.50

Oct. 1912. Complete works. All 1st editions.
135 vols.   Sold, London,   £88

Nov. 4, 1914. Works. Collected set. All 1st ed.
134 vols.   Sold N. Y., $510.00

Feb. 8, 1915. Works. Collected set. All 1st ed. except *Macdermots, Kellys, La Vendée.*
124 vols.   Sold, N. Y., $375.00

March 5, 1915. Works. Collected set. All 1st ed.
134 vols.   Sold, Boston, $536.00

June 3, 1918. Works. Collected set. All 1st ed.
148 vols.   Sold, N. Y., $760.00

March 4, 1919. Collected set. All 1st ed. exc. *Macdermots, Kellys, La Vendée.*
124 vols.   Sold, N. Y., $720.00

April 4, 1921. Works. All 1st ed.
117 vols.   Sold, London, £155

Jan. 26, 1922. Works. Collected set. All 1st ed. exc. one.
135 vols.   Sold, $1,700.00

May 14, 1923. Works. All 1st ed.
129 vols.   Sold, $925.00

May 28, 1923. Works, including *Macdermots,* and a Life of Trollope by T. H. S. Escott, 1913. All 1st ed. exc. one. 1847-1913.
137 vols.   Sold, London, £195

Sept. 12, 1925. McCutcheon, George Barr, Books once were men.

"I bought a set of Trollope (not including the *Macdermots*), neatly rebound in half levant, in about 1903, for $400.00. To-day one has to pay $500.00 or $600.00 for *Macdermots* alone."

In Saturday Evening Post (N. Y.), Sept. 12, 1925, p. 29 and p. 158.

II.—Single Works.

Barchester Towers.

Nov. 11, 1912.	1st ed.	Sold, N. Y. $12.50
May 19, 1915.	1st ed.	Sold, London £1 16s.
Apr. 13, 1921.	1st ed.	Sold, London £3
May 16, 1923.	1st ed.	Sold, London £6
July 10, 1924.	1st ed.	Sold, London £20
July 17, 1924.	1st ed.	Sold, London £16 10s.

Bertrams.

July 10, 1924.	1st ed.	Sold, London £8 10s.

Can you forgive her?

May 3, 1899. 1st ed. Sold, N. Y. $3.25
Mar. 31, 1904. 1st ed. Sold, N. Y. $10.25
Dec. 14, 1909. 1st ed. With one of the original pencil drawings by H. K. Browne, signed, inserted.
Sold, N. Y. $30.00
Nov. 11, 1912. 1st ed. Sold, N. Y. $16.00
Oct. 14, 1919. 1st ed. With autograph letter signed, to Leech. Sold, N. Y. $26.00
Nov. 13, 1919. 1st ed. Sold, London, £2
May 24, 1920. 1st ed. Sold, N. Y. $25.00
Apr. 10, 1922. 1st ed. Author's own copy with bookplate.
Sold, N. Y. $16.00
Feb. 13, 1923. 1st ed. Sold, N. Y. $32.50
Mar. 14, 1923. 1st ed. Sold, London £6 10s.
Jan. 28, 1924. 1st ed. Sold, N. Y. $67.50

Castle Richmond.

Feb. 26, 1901. 1st ed. Sold, N. Y. $3.00
Feb. 5, 1908, 1st ed. Sold, N. Y. $8.00
Mar. 31, 1922. 1st ed. Sold, Phil. $18.00

Framley Parsonage.

Mar. 31, 1922. 1st ed. Sold, Phil. $15.00
Dec. 6. 1922. 1st ed. Sold, London £6 15s.
Nov. 14, 1923. 1st ed. Sold, London £2 16s.

Last chronicle of Barset.

May 31, 1906. 1st ed. Sold, N. Y. $6.50
Mar. 26, 1917. 1st ed. Sold, N. Y. $10.00
Oct. 14, 1917. 1st ed. (?) Sold, N. Y. $17.00
Apr. 20, 1921. 1st ed. (?) Author's presentation copy to Alfred Austin. Sold, N. Y. $55.00
Jan. 22, 1923. 1st ed. Sold, Edinburgh £11
Feb. 13, 1923. 1st ed. Sold, N. Y. $32.50
Mar. 14, 1923. 1st ed. Sold, London, £9
Jan. 28, 1924. 1st ed. Sold, N. Y. $35.00
May. 21 1924. 1st ed. Sold, London £8 5s.

Orley Farm.

Apr. 29, 1903.	1st ed.	Sold, N. Y. $5.00
May 31, 1906.	1st ed.	Sold, N. Y. $6.20
Jan. 18, 1909.	1st ed.	Sold, N. Y. $7.00
June 7, 1910.	1st ed. Author's presentation copy.	
		Sold, N. Y. $5.00
Nov. 11, 1912.	1st ed.	Sold, N. Y. $11.00
Mar. 26, 1914.	1st ed.	Sold, London £1 11s.
Mar. 17, 1919.	1st ed.	Sold, London £1 5s.
Apr. 20, 1921.	Original parts.	Sold, N. Y. $50.00
Mar. 31, 1922.	1st ed.	Sold, Phil. $12.50
Feb. 13, 1923.	Original parts.	Sold, N. Y. $35.00
Mar. 14, 1923.	1st ed.	Sold, London £6
Jan. 28, 1924.	Original parts	Sold, N. Y. $52.50

Phineas Finn.

Feb. 14, 1910.	1st ed. Author's presentation copy.	
		Sold, N. Y. $6.50
Apr. 13, 1921.	1st ed.	Sold, London £1 10s.
Mar. 31, 1922.	1st ed.	Sold, Phil. $19.00

Phineas Redux.

Mar. 31, 1922.	1st ed.	Sold, Phil. $11.00

Prime minister.

Jan. 28, 1924.	1st ed. (?)	Sold, N. Y. $35.00

Ralph the heir.

July 31, 1922.	1st ed.	Sold, London £4 5s.
Jan. 28, 1924.	Original parts.	Sold, N. Y. $45.00

Small House at Allington.

Oct. 2, 1906.	1st ed.	Sold, Boston $3.50
Mar. 31, 1922.	1st ed.	Sold, Phil. $19.00

Three clerks.

Dec. 13, 1905.	1st ed.	Sold, London £1 5s.
July 31, 1907.	1st ed.	Sold, London £2 10s.
Dec. 19, 1912.	1st ed.	Sold, London £4 4s.

La Vendée.

Dec. 13, 1905.	1st ed.	Sold, London £1 5s.

Vicar of Bullhampton.

Jan. 18, 1909.	1st ed.	Sold, N. Y. $5.50
Jan. 24, 1910.	1st ed. With bookplate of Charles Dickens.	
		Sold, N. Y. $14.00
Mar. 17, 1913.	1st ed.	Sold, N. Y. $11.25
Mar. 17, 1919.	1st ed.	Sold, London £1 8s.
June 28, 1921.	1st ed.	Sold, London £1 10s.
Feb. 13, 1923.	1st ed.	Sold, N. Y. $11.00
Jan. 28, 1924.	1st ed.	Sold, N. Y. $25.00